THE GROLIER
LIBRARY OF
World War I

THE GROLIER LIBRARY OF
World War I

1914–17: THE EASTERN FRONT

GROLIER
EDUCATIONAL

Grolier Educational
Grolier Publishing Company, Inc.

This edition first published 1997 for Grolier Educational, Danbury, Connecticut 06816
by Marshall Cavendish Books, an imprint of Times Media Pte Ltd
Times Centre, 1 New Industrial Road, Singapore 536196
Tel: (65) 2848844 Fax: (65) 2854871 Email: te@tpl.com.sg
World Wide Web: http://www.timesone.com.sg/te

Copyright © 1997, 1999, 2001 Times Media Pte Ltd, Singapore
Third Grolier Printing 2001

Set ISBN: 0-7172-9065-4
Volume ISBN: 0-7172-7697-X

Library of Congress Cataloging-in-Publication Data

The Grolier Library of World War I.

p.cm.
Includes bibliographical references and index.
Contents: [1] The causes of conflict — [2] 1914: The race for the sea — [3] 1915: The lines are drawn — [4] 1916: The year
of attrition — [5] 1917: The U.S. enters the war — [6] 1915–17: The Eastern front — [7] 1918: A flawed victory —
[8] 1919–39: The aftermath of war.
Summary: Covers the causes of World War I, the battles and strategy involved, and the aftermath in chronological format.
ISBN 0-7172-9065-4 (hardcover)
1. World War, 1914–1918—Encyclopedias. Juvenile. 2. World War, 1914–1918—Encyclopedias. I Grolier Educational
(Firm).
D522.7.G76 1997
940.3'03—DC21 96–50230
CIP
AC
Printed and bound in Italy

Marshall Cavendish Books
Managing Editor: Ellen Dupont
Project Editor: Tim Cooke
Senior Editor: Sarah Halliwell
Editors: Andrew Brown, Donald Sommerville
Senior Designer: Melissa Stokes
Picture Research: Jeff Cornish, Darren Brasher,
    Ann Hobart-Lang
Editorial Assistant: Lorien Kite
Production: Craig Chubb
Index: Ella J. Skene

Consultant:
Dr. John L. Pimlott,
Head of the Department of War Studies,
The Royal Military Academy Sandhurst,
England.
Text:
Dr. Robert M. Ponichtera,
Yale University,
New Haven, Connecticut.

CONTENTS

The *Grolier Library of World War I* has many features designed to help you find the information you're looking for quickly and get the most out of the books. This page explains how.

Locator maps Use with the main map on pp. 8–9 or the larger maps within the article to find out exactly where the action is taking place.

Eyewitness Firsthand accounts by soldiers and civilians will help you imagine what it might have been like to live through the war.

Date Line An instant guide to the dates and places covered in the article or what aspect of the war it covers, such as Home Front or Sea War.

Biography Brief lives of most of the major characters of the war, both military leaders (The Commanders) and others (War Profiles).

Alternatives "What if...?" features will help you decide for yourself whether or not the men running the war could have done things differently.

Larger maps show places of particular interest in more detail. With the locator maps at the start of each article, they help you understand where things happened.

Factfiles An at-a-glance summary of each major battle. Because many casualty figures from the war are inaccurate, they are meant as a guide only; they usually include dead and wounded.

Features Highlight interesting aspects of the war and discuss them in more detail. They are grouped in categories: women; weapons; tactics; the home front; new inventions; behind the lines; the armies; men of the future; and politics.

Where to Find Every article ends by telling you where you can find related topics. Use them to read in more detail about different aspects of a subject or to learn how different incidents and people relate to each other.

Maps: Each volume begins with a world map on pages 8–9 to show you the location of the action covered in the book.

Contents: Pages 5–6 of each volume list all the subjects covered in the book, as well as every feature, biography, and background entry. Boxes and biographies are marked in italics; more general background entries are highlighted in bold.

Background Features: These pages, easily found because of their entries' shaded background, deal in detail with important subjects related to the articles they follow.

Glossary & Bibliography: At the back of the book is a glossary that explains words often used in the set. A bibliography lists other books you can read about World World I.

Index: An index that covers the entire set appears in each volume.

1914-17: The Eastern Front

The war in the east was fought along a front hundreds of miles long, from the Baltic in the north to the Carpathian Mountains in the south. After the Russians invaded German East Prussia and Austrian Galicia in 1914, the Central Powers pushed them back during the next three years. Much of the fighting took place in what is now Poland, where the Poles saw the war as a chance to gain their independence. The Czech and Slovak peoples also wanted to create their own nation.

When peace came in 1917, the Central Powers occupied territory deep inside Russia. They lost their gains after the western Allies defeated them in 1918. Poland and Czechoslovakia gained their independence in the peace settlements.

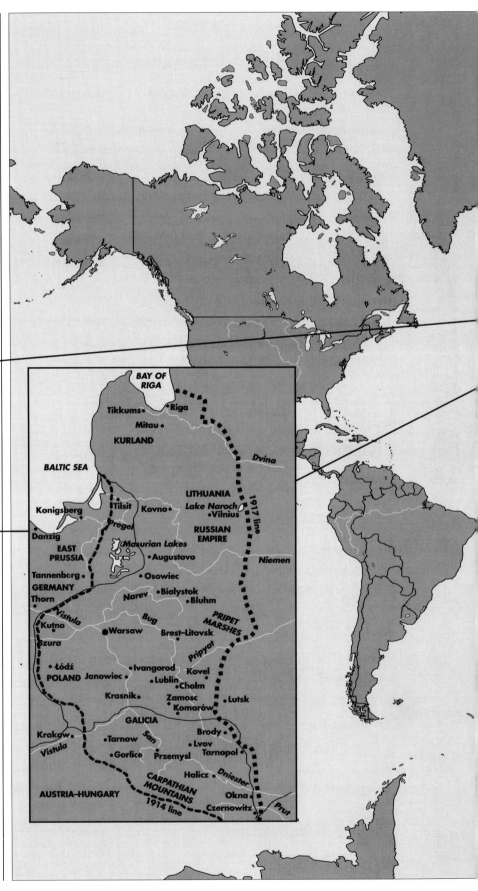

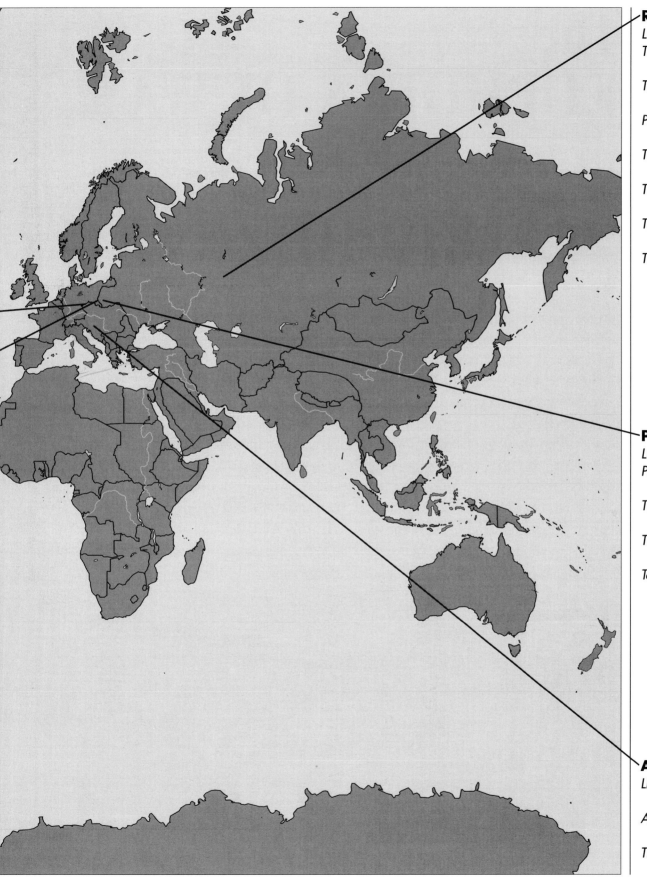

The EUPHORIA OF WAR

As the world hovered on the brink of war, a wave of patriotism swept Eastern Europe.

On July 25, 1914, Russia mobilized in support of Serbia against Austria-Hungary. Germany in turn declared war on Russia on August 1. The Russian people responded eagerly to the challenge of war. Days after Russia's declaration of war a patriotic Russian mob ransacked the German embassy in the capital, St. Petersburg. The name of the capital was changed from the German-sounding "Petersburg" to Petrograd. And factory workers abandoned their riots over poor job conditions and began demonstrating in support of Serbia. The Russian people declared their allegiance to the czar in the upcoming struggle against the Germans.

Similar reactions arose in Austria-Hungary. News of the decision to wage war against Russia generated spontaneous celebrations in the streets of Vienna, with people displaying pictures of their emperor, Franz Josef, and waving black and yellow Hapsburg flags.

The empire rallies to war

Even the multiethnic peoples subject to the great Eastern European empires generally welcomed war. The Austro-Hungarian Empire consisted not only of Germans and Hungarians but also Poles, Czechs, Bosnians, Serbs, Croats, Slovaks, Romanians, and others. Polish crowds in

A prowar demonstration taking place in a Russian city in 1914.

Citizens of Budapest, capital of Hungary, read the Austro-Hungarian mobilization order that will send their soldiers to the battlefields.

Warsaw now cheered on Russian soldiers – the same Russians who had violently put down three Polish uprisings during the previous 120 years. Only the Czechs did not seem to welcome the outbreak of war. Just the same, the vast majority of Czech political parties gave their support to the Austrian monarchy.

Patriotism, the desire to punish the aggressor – Serbia in Austria's eyes, Austria in Russia's eyes – and the prospect of a relatively painless victory motivated these displays of early popular support. And even if this enthusiasm was short-lived, people in general accepted the call to fight. Some joined because they thought it was their duty to serve the state; others,

like the peasantry, because it was yet another obligation to fulfill. There was little outright antiwar sentiment. Generally speaking, people did what their leaders asked of them.

Yet much prewar feeling was closely connected with the belief that the war would be a short one. As the conflict dragged on, and casualties and hardships at home mounted, the people of Eastern Europe would become less and less tolerant of their governments. Ultimately ethnic and social tensions, aggravated by war-weariness, would provoke radical political change, toppling the empires of Eastern Europe even before they could finish the war that they had been so willing to start.

The Battle of
TANNENBERG

The Russians' first battle against the Germans brought bloody slaughter and chaotic retreat for the czar's forces.

A group of Russian peasants is conscripted to fight in the war. These people had little choice in joining the war; they simply had to follow the czar's orders.

T he Russians and the Germans first clashed at Tannenberg in East Prussia, inside the easternmost part of German territory. During this battle a German force surrounded and annihilated the Russian Second Army. It was one of the greatest German victories of the war.

This triumph would prevent the Russians from advancing into East Prussia. The battle opened the long and painful process of the war in the east.

According to the German war plan, completed by Count Alfred von Schlieffen in 1906, the German army's priority in

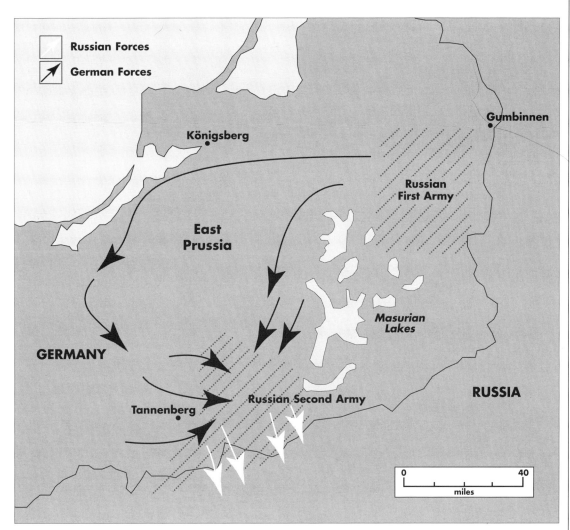

August 1914 was the Western Front. The German army would concentrate its strength westward in the hope of rapidly defeating the French. A much smaller force would be left to defend East Prussia. Germany had always thought that Russia would take at least six weeks to get its army ready for war. But the Russians surprised them. Under pressure from their French allies, who feared the immense weight of a German offensive in the west, they mobilized ahead of schedule and attacked from the east.

On August 15 the Russian First Army, under General Paweł Rennenkampf, marched into East Prussia from the east.

FactFile

OPPOSING FORCES	German: 13 infantry divisions, one cavalry division	Russian: 21 infantry divisions, nine and one half cavalry divisions
COMMANDERS	Eighth Army: Hindenburg; Chief of Staff: Ludendorff	Northwest Army Group: Zhilinski; First Army: Rennenkampf; Second Army: Samsonov
LOCATION	37-mile front to the southwest of Allenstein (Olsztyn) in East Prussia (Germany)	
DURATION	August 26 – 30, 1914	
OUTCOME	The advance of the Russian army into East Prussia is halted.	
CASUALTIES	German: 12,000	Russian: 92,000 captured; 50,000 killed or wounded

Paul von Hindenburg 1847–1934
German general and politician
Of an old military family, Paul von Beneckendorff und Hindenburg served in the Franco-Prussian war of 1870 to 1871 and later became a general. Brought out of retirement to replace the disgraced Prittwitz, Hindenburg became a popular hero in Germany as a result of the victory at Tannenberg. Over the next two years he and his chief of staff Ludendorff won a series of victories on the Eastern Front. In 1916 he became chief of the general staff and, together with Ludendorff, dictated German strategy for the remainder of the war. Though Hindenburg was officially the head of this partnership, Ludendorff was the real brains.

Hindenburg was elected president of Germany in 1925 and remained in office until his death in 1934. By the time he died Hitler and the Nazis had formed their first government.

Paul von Hindenburg on the Eastern Front. The general would become a major figure in the Germans' Russian campaign.

Five days later, General Aleksandr Samsonov's Second Army entered German territory from the south. They intended to surround and capture the German defenders – or to drive them from East Prussia altogether. If the two Russian armies could link up, they could then spearhead a drive on the German capital, Berlin.

But the Russians had a tough task. The land they had to cross was cluttered with dense forests, lakes, and marshlands. From the south, there were few roads and even fewer railroad lines. There were also difficulties with provisions. Their supply service could not provide for all their thousands of men; rations often arrived at the wrong unit, or got lost altogether.

A lack of communication

Russian problems did not end there. The men running the war often clashed over how to fight the war. Many Russian officers were old and lazy, having gained their positions through wealth or social position rather than military skill. Communication between the armies was also a problem. The intelligence system was poor and there were problems with the wireless. Contact between the two Russian armies was limited. In any case, Samsonov and Rennenkampf refused to talk to each other: they had fallen out in 1905. They had no idea about the plans and movements of the enemy.

A bold attack

By contrast, German intelligence was excellent. The leader of the German Eighth Army, General Max von Prittwitz, already knew that he was facing two enemy

Generalfeldmarschall von Hindenburg im Osten

inventions

Radio

The wireless revolutionized war communications. It was vital that commanders kept in contact in order to coordinate their tactics, and the wireless was a quick and reliable method.

But enemies and allies alike criticized the Russians' ineffective use of the wireless: Rather than concealing messages by code like other armies, Russian army units usually spoke plainly. By intercepting these transmissions, the Germans could easily discover their plans.

In addition the Russians could not obtain the amount of telephone wire they needed to establish adequate communications. And most importantly, there weren't enough codebooks to go around. This meant that if one Russian sent a concealed message to another, the recipient could not decode it. The Russians could not afford to be unaware of the position of their own forces, so they broadcast without code and risked interception. This was a fatal error. It gave the Germans an enormous advantage in crushing Samsonov at Tannenberg.

A German radio station on the Eastern Front. The Germans' superior communications helped them to win at Tannenberg.

Soldiers of the czar's army on their way to the front, 1914.

EYEWITNESS

A contemporary German account related the brutal horrors of the battle. An eyewitness, an officer returning from Tannenberg, said that the horrors he saw there would live in his dreams until his dying day:

66 The sight of thousands of Russians driven into two huge lakes or swamps to drown was ghastly, and the shrieks and cries of the dying men and horses he will never forget. So fearful was the sight of these thousands of men with their guns, horses and ammunition struggling in the water, that, to shorten their agony, they [the Germans] turned their machine guns on them.... And the mowing down of the cavalry brigade at the same time, 500 mounted men on white horses, all killed and packed so closely together that they remained standing ... [t]his sight was the ghastliest of the whole war. **99**

doning most of East Prussia to the Russians. Then he changed his mind and decided that withdrawal was not necessary. But his pessimism had sealed his fate. Moltke, the German army's chief of staff, had no time for talk of retreat and fired him.

A new team

Moltke needed someone calm and bold to replace the disgraced Prittwitz. He found his ideal candidate in a 68-year-old general currently in retirement. General Paul von Hindenburg arrived on the Eastern Front on August 23, together with a new chief of staff, Erich Ludendorff, a hero of the invasion of Belgium in the West. Together they would prove a formidable team.

By now the Eighth Army staff had come up with a new plan: to tie down Rennenkampf's army with a small decoy force and

forces. On August 20, intelligence told him that Rennenkampf's army was advancing. Prittwitz decided to attack at once. He wanted to crush the Russian First Army before Samsonov could even arrive.

But Prittwitz's plan did not work. When he attacked on August 20 at a village called Gumbinnen, the Russians repelled his forces. Although this was no more than a minor setback, Prittwitz panicked. He telephoned supreme headquarters back in Berlin to request a withdrawal of German forces across the Vistula River, thus aban-

THE COMMANDERS

Aleksandr Vassilevich Samsonov 1859–1914
Russian general
A career officer with a distinguished record of service, Samsonov was a graduate of the renowned Nikolaevskoe General Staff Academy. He served capably as commander of a cavalry division during the Russo–Japanese War in 1904 and 1905, as chief of staff of the Warsaw Military District, and as the governor-general of Turkestan.

For his service he was nearly appointed Northwest Army Group commander over Zhilinski. He shot himself in despair over his staggering defeat at Tannenberg. His reputation was tarnished by his performance at the battle.

General Aleksandr Samsonov. Crushed after his defeat at Tannenberg, the ruined Russian general shot himself.

direct the bulk of the German strength against Samsonov.

After the successful Russian defense at Gumbinnen, the Russian high command assumed that the enemy had retreated. They ordered Samsonov to keep advancing in order to cut off the Germans they believed he would find in front of him. But the Russians had guessed wrong about the German strategy. The Germans had switched troops from the positions opposite Rennenkampf to face Samsonov, moving their army by rail. Meanwhile, two more German corps were also marching on the Russian Second Army. The Germans would strike from all sides.

As the Germans waited to spring their trap Samsonov pushed forward even further. The Germans attacked on August 27. The following day, as they closed in, Samsonov ordered a general retreat. By August 29 the Russian army was surrounded. Nearly all roads of retreat had been cut. Scenes of horrific slaughter followed, as entrapped Russians desperately tried to break through the German lines. Even some German troops reputedly went crazy during the fight, as they fired over and over again into the terrified Russian masses.

The end of a general

The proud and dedicated Samsonov, his reputation in ruins, was numbed by the scale of his defeat. In the chaos of the Russian retreat and with night falling, he and his staff found themselves stranded in a thick, swampy forest just seven miles from the Russian border. Around midnight the broken general wandered off alone through the trees. Moments later a gunshot rang out in the darkness. One of the most senior officers in the Russian army had killed himself.

While Samsonov could not face the enormity of his defeat, the Germans could not believe the staggering scale of their victory. By August 30 they had captured 400 guns, and 92,000 Russian survivors. Sent to a prisoner of war camp outside of Berlin, the captives received starvation rations and slept in barracks that were freezing cold. The first had died by Christ-mas 1914, and many more would follow as the war went on.

Meanwhile the men of Rennenkampf's First Army, unaware of the terrible slaughter, continued to cool their heels. Hampered again by their poor communications, the Russian high command did not fully realize what had happened until September 2, days after the battle was over.

Back home, news of the defeat stunned the citizens of Petrograd. One officer recalled how a distressed and shaken crowd gathered before army headquarters waiting for news. "What a disaster!" a voice cried out, "Even generals have been killed! Why is the government deceiving us with news of victories?" Rumors circulated about the horrible fate of the Russian army. One thing was clear: No one had escaped the German trap.

A German newspaper dated August 29, 1914, tells of good news from the front.

In Groß-Berlin 5 Pf.

B·Z am Mittag

Nr. 204		1 Uhr
Berliner Zeitung		Sonnabend
38. Jahrgang		29. August 1914

Verlag Ullstein & Co. Redaktion: Berlin SW 68, Kochstraße 22–25. Abonnement: Monatlich 1,20 M. In Berlin frei ins Haus. Außerhalb bei der Post. Zusendung unter Streifband wöchentlich 60 Pfennig, Ausland 90 Pfennig. Einzelnummer 5 Pfennig, außerhalb 10 Pfennig.

Anzeigen: Die sechsgespaltene Nonparelle - Zeile 75 Pfennig. Reklamezeile 5 Mark. Annahmeschluß für Anzeigen am Tage zuvor bis 6 Uhr abends. Telegramm-Adresse: Ullsteinhaus Berlin. Telephon-Zentrale: Ullstein & Co. Amt Moritzplatz, Nr. 11300 bis 11345.

Freudenbotschaft aus Ostpreußen:

Fünf russische Armeekorps geschlagen.

Wolffs Telegraphen-Bureau meldet amtlich:

Berlin, 29. August.

Unsere Truppen in Preußen unter Führung des Generalobersten von Hindenburg haben die vom Narew vorgegangene russische Armee in der Stärke von fünf Armeekorps und drei Kavalleriedivisionen in dreitägiger Schlacht in der Gegend von Gilgenburg und Ortelsburg geschlagen und verfolgen sie jetzt über die Grenze.

Der Generalquartiermeister
von Stein.

A staggering victory

In contrast, news of the victory was celebrated across Germany. The press, desperately in need of heroes – the campaign on the Western Front was not going well – hailed Hindenburg and Ludendorff as geniuses. Indeed to many Germans, including these two leaders, it now seemed that the war could be won in the east. They urged that the high command should abandon the Schlieffen Plan and channel the necessary resources against Russia.

Yet while Tannenberg was a dramatic defeat for the armies of Czar Nicholas II, it was not a decisive one. Although their losses were tremendous – almost 150,000 men captured, killed, or wounded – they counted for only a fraction of the total Russian forces. And within weeks the Russians would invade East Prussia again.

August 1914
by Aleksandr Solzhenitsyn

Russian author Aleksandr Solzhenitsyn's mammoth novel, published in 1989, portrays the Russian army in East Prussia during the Battle of Tannenberg. It is a stinging attack on Russia's military and political leadership. The author's sympathies lie with the common soldier, who faces his destiny with heroic strength. In contrast, Solzhenitsyn depicts the leadership of the Russian armies on the Eastern Front as cowardly and confused, incapacitated by a stifling bureaucracy.

The leaders of the Russian state and army earned Solzhenitsyn's wrath not only for the way they were running the war but for plunging the country into the conflict in the first place. The author passionately believed that the slow and steady economic development in Russia since the turn of the 20th century would have continued, bringing prosperity and stability to the Russian people, had war not intervened.

While *August 1914* is a powerful and vivid account of the people and events of Russian history, it expresses the author's personal opinions rather than strict historical fact. In reality, although poor leadership contributed to the Russian defeat at Tannenberg, structural weaknesses within the army, the initial inability to understand the nature of modern warfare, and even German luck were equally responsible for the final outcome.

WHERE TO FIND...

Life in RUSSIA

Unrest among workers at home and soldiers at the front threatened to cause problems for the czar.

Armed citizens man a barricade in a Russian city. This was just one of the rebellions that occurred as the Russian people heard news of "Bloody Sunday," the murder of hundreds of citizens in St. Petersburg in January 1905: Trouble broke out throughout the country.

In imperial Russia the initial enthusiasm for the war provided the monarchy with a golden opportunity to create the illusion of national unity. And since the army achieved some successes during the first ten months of the war, many opponents of government policies withheld their criticisms for the sake of the war effort. Several political leaders also dedicated their energies to the war, organizing industrial enterprises. These provided the army with boots, tents, and medical services.

Civic groups also came forward to contribute. It slowly became clear that these organizations were more capable and efficient than the government. Their own successes prompted them, by 1915, to seek political concessions from the czar. Above

all they wanted a government responsible to parliament. But Nicholas II was not interested in such changes.

There was tension beneath Russia's surface. The majority of peasants reported for duty in the army only out of obligation. Military service was seen as a misfortune. Peasants had no choice but to submit to the czar's orders and fight.

The growing dissatisfaction of workers was a cause for alarm. The people had risen up against injustice before: In 1905 strikes had paralyzed Russia's economy. Nicholas could not afford for that to happen now. Inflation and bleak working conditions now prompted strikes, to which the government responded with force. And as 1915 began, with demands for additional sacrifices, the problems of the Russian home front could only get worse.

Left: Russian peasants typical of those conscripted to fight in the Russian army. Most did not even know why they were fighting and joined only because they were forced to. Nearly 15 million men served in the Russian army during the war.

home front

Industrialization

The ultimate collapse of czarist Russia is often blamed on its inability to modernize its industry. Russia is often seen as an inefficient giant that could not produce enough weaponry.

Industrialization in Russia was problematic. The most modern equipment, imported from Western Europe, was frequently operated by an unskilled labor force. And after 1914 workers struggled to meet the increased demand. The need for war material forced women and children into the factories.

Yet Russian industry was far from a liability. Although it lagged behind the rest of Europe, Russia had still enjoyed industrial growth before the war. When the government finally realized the requirements of modern warfare, industry rose to the occasion. By 1916 it was producing enough to contribute to a victorious war effort. Yet it was a strain to do so – a strain that would have serious consequences in 1917.

The Battle of ZAMOSC-KOMARÓW

As the Russians managed to push the Austrians back from their own province of Galicia, the Austrians began to question the loyalty of their German allies.

For the Russians the battle of Zamosc-Komarów turned out to be a welcome contrast to the crippling defeat at Tannenberg. The Russians were facing the forces of Austria-Hungary for the first time, in the enemy territory of Galicia, but they would snatch back the advantage, forcing the enemy into a 150-mile retreat.

Faced with two enemies – Russia to the east and Serbia to the south – Austria-Hungary was forced to fight a two-front war. Emperor Franz Josef's German allies wanted him to concentrate on fighting Russia in order to cover the scant German forces battling the Russians in East Prussia. The Austrian chief of staff, General Franz Conrad von Hötzendorf, left the largest part of his army to face the Russians, but in late July he also sent 12 divisions southward against Serbia.

At the last moment, however, Conrad changed his mind and tried to send these forces back to fight the Russians in Galicia instead. But confusion on the inefficient railroads and primitive communications slowed their progress. Parts of the Second Army were still on the move even as the Austrians struck.

Initial success for Conrad

At first it seemed as though the Austrians would not need their additional troops after all. Three days later the Austrian Fourth Army under Auffenberg attacked in the area of Zamosc-Komarów – two Polish towns in Russia, across the border from Austrian Galicia. They succeeded in partially enveloping Russia's Fifth Army, led by General Plehve. Yet unlike Russian General Samsonov, who had marched into his encirclement at Tannenberg, Plehve

FactFile

OPPOSING FORCES	Austro-Hungarian: 37 infantry divisions, 10 cavalry divisions, 2 German divisions	Russian: 53 and one half infantry divisions, 18 cavalry divisions
COMMANDERS	C o S: Conrad; Fourth Army: Auffenberg	Third Army: Ruzski; Fourth Army: Evert; Fifth Army: Plehve; Eighth Army: Brusilov
LOCATION	A 175-mile front stretching from south of Lublin to the Dniester River north of Stanislavov in Austrian Galicia	
DURATION	August 26 – 31, 1914	
OUTCOME	Russian army repels Austrian attack. Nearly all of Austrian Galicia falls into Russian hands.	
CASUALTIES	Austrian: 100,000 captured; 300,000 killed or wounded	Russian: 40,000 captured; 210,000 killed or wounded

promptly ordered a retreat. The Austrian attackers, exhausted, did not press forward to finish the job.

Defeat for the Russians

The Austrians won the battle. Plehve had lost 40 percent of his forces, while the Russian Fourth Army under Evert had been severely battered in the opening fighting. Elsewhere, however, the Austrians were not so lucky. To the southeast of the fortress of Lvov (Lemberg) – Galicia's capital – another Austrian commander, General Brudermann, plowed his army into the whole of Ruzski's Third Army between August 26 and 28. He had wrongly assumed that the opponent facing him was "an isolated corps." The Austrians took heavy losses before falling back, regrouping at the Gnila Lipa River. Here, despite being reinforced by the newly arrived Second Army, Conrad's forces were over-

Russian troops move forward through barbed-wire defenses.

come by the oncoming Third and Eighth Russian armies, and suffered still more crippling casualties. The Austrians fled to Lvov but soon abandoned it. On September 3 Ruzski marched into the city.

Overwhelming the Austrians

Despite impending disaster, Conrad refused to cut his losses. He had heard that the German Eighth Army had just won an impressive victory in East Prussia and was determined to show that the Austrians could do the same. Conrad intended to throw Auffenberg's Fourth Army against the flanks of the advancing Russian Third and Eighth. But the Russians changed the direction of their march, meeting the

Austrians head on. In the following clash the Austrian troops held their own, but to the north a swelling tide of Russian troops – including Plehve's Fifth Army, which had regrouped quickly after their retreat at Komarów – overwhelmed the Austrian flank, and the front collapsed.

Conrad falls back

On September 11 Conrad ordered a general retreat to the San River, some 60 miles to the rear. The Russians continued to advance. But the Austrians quickly discovered – thanks once more to intercepted radio messages – that Russia's Fourth Army was now bearing down from the north. Leaving behind some 150,000 troops

A Russian soldier reloads his gun as he lies in ambush in 1914.

to defend the fortress of Przemysl, Conrad's forces fell back yet another 80 miles to the Dunajec River, east of Kraków. The retreat led some of the more pessimistic residents of Austria's capital, Vienna, to remark that the ultimate strategy of the Austrian high command was "simply to tire the invaders out."

A damaging defeat

With this defeat the Russians managed to drive the Austrian armies from all of Austrian Galicia except for the Austro-Hungarian fortress of Przemysl. The Austrians had lost many irreplaceable junior officers and NCOs – noncommissioned officers – and overall morale was severely damaged.

Lasting frictions flared up between the Austrians and their German allies. Conrad, wiring for help as he retreated, was curtly informed that the German Eighth Army could do no more than it had already done to help the Austrians. Irritated that the Germans did not transfer troops eastward after their own offensive had stalled in the west, Conrad even began to wonder if his

Austrian Chief of Staff Franz Conrad von Hötzendorf studies a map. Conrad was a bold and imaginative leader who became frustrated by what he saw as a lack of support from his German allies.

allies were seeking a separate peace with the Russians. On their side the Germans began to doubt the fighting value of their Austrian partners. A pattern of mutual recrimination between the allies had begun, and it would only worsen as the war raged on.

EYEWITNESS

Friedrich Feuchtinger, a soldier in the Austrian reserves, recalled his unit's attack on a Russian position:

66 The Russians turned to flee. One of them, being closely chased, and apparently without his rifle, stopped all of a sudden, turned around, held out his right hand, and put his left hand into his tunic pocket. As he did so, I plunged in my bayonet. I see his blood redden his uniform, hear him moan and groan as he twists with the bayonet in his young body. I am seized with terror. I throw myself down, crawl to him, wanting to help him. But he is dead. I pull my bloodstained bayonet from the dead body. Wanting to fold his hands, I see in the left hand a crumpled photo of his wife and child. **99**

WHERE TO FIND...

Franz Conrad von Hötzendorf: 4:50

Railroads: 3:13

Siege of Przemysl: 6:30

Austrian-German Tensions: 6:57

Austrian prisoners trudge toward captivity.

Life in AUSTRIA-HUNGARY

Austria-Hungary was made up of many different ethnic groups. Would the war bring them together or increase the differences between them and tear the empire apart?

Far right: The city of Budapest, capital of Hungary, on the Danube River.

For the other Great Powers of Europe the Hapsburg Empire of Austria-Hungary was both a marvel and a cause for concern. On the one hand the continent wondered at Emperor Franz Josef's ability to keep his empire in one piece. Although its traditional rulers were Germans and Hungarians, the empire included people from a great many ethnic groups: Czechs, Slovaks, Poles, Ukrainians, Jews, Serbs, Croats, Slovenes, Romanians, and Italians.

On the other hand Europeans assumed that, sooner or later, ethnic tensions would tear Austria apart. If this happened, either Russia or Germany would probably gain political influence – perhaps even territory – in the Balkans. With the Balkans' important position between the Mediterranean and the Black Sea, linking Europe with Greece and the Ottoman Empire, such a change would threaten the interests of the other European countries.

Complicated loyalties

Austria-Hungary may have been close to disintegrating when the war began. The empire's Croats wanted to end their political association with the Hungarians; Czechs and Germans quarreled bitterly over language laws; and Serbs looked abroad to Serbia for support. Yet people of all nationalities felt a certain loyalty to the aged emperor, Franz Josef. Even the most vocal opponents of the Austrian and Hungarian governments supported the war effort in 1914.

One symbol of the monarchy's strength was the army. Although many officers were German, Poles, Czechs, and Croats gladly made military service a career. To encourage unity officers had to speak the same language as the soldiers in their units, not the other way around.

When the war began, some people thought that it would only postpone the inevitable breakup of the empire. Others thought that it might halt Austria-Hungary's development toward becoming a federation, with all its peoples having an equal share in creating government policy. Ultimately the war would force the empire to shatter into pieces, as the ethnic states claimed their independence.

HOME FRONT

Austria-Hungary

WAR PROFILES

Stephen Tisza 1857–1918

Hungarian prime minister

The son of a prime minister, Stephen Tisza worked throughout his political career to further the interests of the Hungarian people. He served as prime minister in the government of Hungary from 1903 to 1905 and again from 1913 to 1917.

Tisza agreed to Hungarian participation in World War I only after the Austrians promised not to annex Serbian territory. Tisza believed that if additional Slavic peoples were brought into the empire, this would endanger the status of the Hungarians.

Tisza opposed universal suffrage and equal rights for non-Hungarians. On October 31, 1918, Tisza was murdered by Red Guards in Budapest.

WHERE TO FIND...

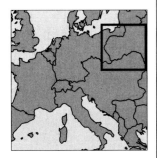

*One of the defenders'
concrete gun positions
looks out from the
fortress of Przemysl. The
Austrians blew up most
of the guns before they
surrendered in
March 1915.*

The Siege of
PRZEMYSL

Winter battles were fought to relieve a surrounded Austrian
fortress but in the end the starving garrison had to surrender.

Victory at the battle of Zamosc-Komarów left the Russians occupying the whole of the Austrian province of Galicia – except the fortress of Przemysl. The stronghold became a symbol of Austrian resistance. But its defenders faced a bitter struggle. After five months they gave in, defeated not only by the Russians, but also by starvation and illness.

Przemysl had been built specifically to guard against a Russian attack across the Austro-Hungarian border. And if the invaders tried to bypass the fortress into Galicia – today mainly in southern Poland – railroads would enable the Przemysl garrison to disrupt the advance. The Russians needed to capture the fortress.

A city under siege
As the Austrians retreated from Galicia in September 1914 the Russians trapped some 145,000 people – 120,000 troops and

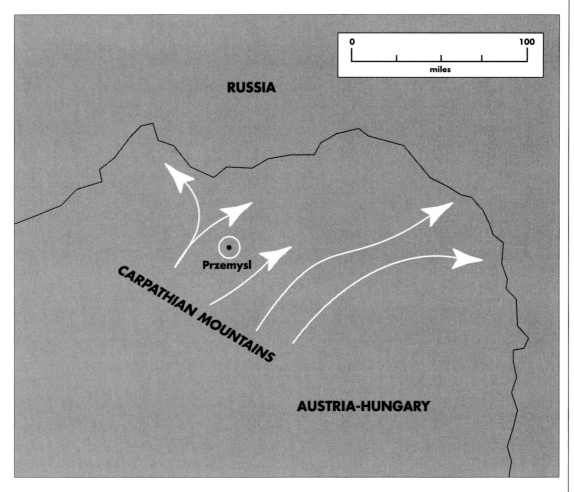

RUSSIA

Przemysl

CARPATHIAN MOUNTAINS

AUSTRIA-HUNGARY

0   100
miles

The white arrows on the map show the advance of the Austrians and Germans through Galicia from May to October 1915. The map shows how important it was for both sides to hold Przemysl.

25,000 civilians – in Przemysl. The fortress had formidable defenses but only limited supplies of food and ammunition. A month after the siege began Austrian forces attacked and pushed the Russians back, enabling them to deliver supplies. But by November 1914 the Russians had advanced and cut off the fortress again.

Despite heavy casualties and shortages of equipment, Field Marshal Conrad, the Austrian commander in chief, ordered immediate attacks to relieve Przemysl. He was worried that if the garrison fell, Italy and Romania would think that Austria-Hungary was losing the war and would join the Allies. That would hit Austria hard. During the winter of 1914 and into the new year, Przemysl was the target of a series of attacks and counterattacks as the Russian and Austrian armies fought in the Carpathian Mountains.

Both Conrad and his Russian counterparts urged their men on, but a lack of roads, bitter cold temperatures, and deep snow created wretched fighting conditions. Both sides paid dearly for little gain. Thousands of men died. Some were killed by the enemy, but most froze to death on the mountain ridges.

All of Conrad's attempts to relieve Przemysl were a failure. By February the Russians had increased their artillery bombardment of the fortress. The defenders had begun to eat their horses as food got short.

By March 1915 the Austrian commander in Przemysl knew that he either had to

Russian prisoners line up for inspection after the Austrians had captured them when they retook Przemysl in June 1915. The second photograph shows them after they have been washed, disinfected, and given new clothes.

break out or surrender. All the food supplies had been used up; many of his men were sick; and all relief attempts had failed. On March 18 the Austrians in the fortress made a last-ditch effort to break out. The Russians drove them back. Three days later the defenders destroyed all their equipment. On March 22, 1915, they surrendered to the Russians.

The campaign to relieve Przemysl cost the Austrians some 800,000 casualties and the collapse of the fortress left the Russians poised for an offensive into Hungary. Austria-Hungary would now have to call on yet more help from Germany.

In early April the Germans transferred troops from France to the region. They were just in time. The Austrians had suffered heavy defeats as the Russians pushed through the Carpathian Mountains. But by April 10 the Austro-German force had halted their advance. The Central Powers could now prepare for an offensive of their own, beginning in May 1915, that would push the Russians out of Galicia for good and allow them to recapture Przemysl.

EYEWITNESS

A Romanian reserve officer fought in the Austrian army in the Carpathian campaign. The following entry is from his diary, dated October 30-31, 1914:

66 On the 30th I witnessed a horrid scene in the trenches. Some 20 men of the 1st Company, commanded by the engineer Weindl, were punished for eating their reserve rations. ... The 'delinquents' were lined up in a row and beaten, one by one, from behind by the sergeant major. Each man who quailed before these brutal blows and staggered forward under their weight was immediately smitten on the head or full in the face until he bled. Some fell in a heap, others went down on their knees and begged their tormentors not to kill them. The reply was redoubled and more ferocious vigor in the blows. Next day half of them were sent down to the doctor, and I don't know what became of them. 99

German troops march a column of Russian prisoners through Przemysl. The city's recapture would come in June 1915 as the Central Powers swept the Russians back out of Galicia.

politics

National aspirations

One of the repercussions of a war pitting Russia against Austria-Hungary was the possibility of a change in the status of the Poles, Czechs, Slovaks, and other nationalities living within the borders of the two empires. Some, like the Poles and the Czechs, had a long history that included periods with their own independent states. Others, like the Slovaks, had never had the opportunity to rule themselves. Before the war, the leaders of these peoples had tried to strengthen the position of their compatriots within the two empires. Some called, for example, for the right to teach in the schools in their native languages and to use them in legal and government matters. Others had different plans and simply demanded their independence.

For their part the Austro-Hungarians and Russians tried to use the various nationalities against their enemies. As the war progressed, the subject nationalities saw an opportunity to win real changes, and became more determined than ever to achieve this. At the same time the power of the multinational empires to curb them grew weaker and weaker.

RUSSIA

GERMANY

• Łódź

AUSTRIA-HUNGARY

The Battle of
ŁÓDŹ

Around the town of Łódź, the Germans would foil a Russian invasion but come dangerously close to a serious defeat.

After the fall of Łódź Russian citizens, fearful of what the Germans might do, try to withdraw their money from one of the local banks.

FactFile

OPPOSING FORCES	German: 250,000	Russian: approx. 500,000 – 600,000
COMMANDERS	Ninth Army: Mackensen	Northwest Army Group: Ruzski; First Army: Rennenkampf; Second Army: Schneidemann; Fifth Army: Plehve
LOCATION	Central Poland	
DURATION	November 11 – 26, 1914	
OUTCOME	Russian attempt to invade Germany halted.	
CASUALTIES	German: 100,000	Russian: 100,000

In November 1914 Russian forces in what is now central Poland prepared to cross the German border and attack the province of Silesia. But before they could, a German attack forced the Russians onto the defensive around the Polish town of Łódź. The German attack began well, but then heavy losses and a lack of ammunition brought it to a halt.

At the start of November the German generals Hindenburg and Ludendorff were confident that they could win a decisive victory on the Eastern Front. Early the previous month their Eighth Army had defeated the Russian First Army commanded by General Pavel Rennenkampf at the Masurian Lakes. Despite heavy casualties, the Germans had driven the Russians from East Prussia. They had even advanced into Russia itself, only to be driven back after ten days.

Russia's military commanders squabbled among themselves about how best to retaliate. By late September they had decided to launch a full–scale offensive from their Polish territory into Germany.

A counterattack

The Germans and Austrians had a plan of their own. They could thwart the Russian offensive, they believed, if they could counter it with their own attack, one that might end the war in the east before win-

---

the armies

Cossacks

The Cossacks, a people of the steppe region between the Dneiper and Don rivers, were originally runaway peasants who, over the centuries, were recruited to fight for the Russian czars. Known for their skill as horsemen, the Cossacks generally served in the cavalry and horse artillery. They also had a reputation for fierceness, as an

Austrian cavalryman could attest: "I was really lucky to escape with my life yesterday," he wrote to a friend in 1915, "because the Cossacks show no mercy if they catch you!"

But the Cossacks' traditional ways of fighting on horseback were becoming out of date. During the Russo–Japanese War from 1904 to 1905 small numbers of Japanese soldiers, equipped with modern weaponry inflicted heavy casualties on the Cossacks. The same thing happened when the Cossacks fought modern armies during World War I, limiting their use as a fighting force. During the Russian Revolution most Cossacks fought on the side of the anticommunist Whites, but they later served in both the Red and White forces during the civil war.

In their distinctive hats, Cossack horsemen make their way along a Russian road. The Cossacks' uniforms were still based on the traditional clothing of their people.

ter. But the attack did not begin well. A spearhead force from the German Ninth Army attacked Warsaw in central Poland on October 9. Only 11 days later, however, they had to withdraw. Meanwhile the Russians dealt the Austrians another defeat to the southeast, inflicting 40,000 casualties at the Battle of Ivangorod.

A celebrated team

On November 1 the newly promoted Field Marshal Paul von Hindenburg became the commander of all the German armies in the east. Although Hindenburg had been hailed as the "savior of East Prussia" for his success at Tannenberg, his chief of staff, Erich Ludendorff, was the real decision maker. Together they made a formidable team. They called for increased forces to face the expected Russian offensive into German Silesia. The plea fell on deaf ears. The German commander in chief, Falkenhayn, wanted to concentrate his men on the Western Front. Ludendorff would have to make do with what he had.

Surprise attack

From intercepted radio messages, the German generals learned of a weak point in the forces facing them, the right flank of the Russian Second Army. They decided to strike. They rapidly shifted a whole army – 250,000 men – by rail from central Poland almost 200 miles north into East Prussia.

On November 11 this Ninth Army – led by General August von Mackensen – fell on the startled Russians, scattering some of Rennenkampf's troops. The right wing of the Second Army proved as weak as the Germans hoped: within four days they pushed it back over 40 miles. The Russians

quickly retreated to the town of Łódź, their supply center for the area.

Now it was the Germans' turn to miscalculate. Ludendorff, assuming that the Russians were in headlong retreat, pressed on toward Łódź. In snow and freezing rain a German corps swung around the city in order to block the fleeing Russians. But the Russian Second Army still held on around the town, while the Fifth Army moved up

Germans guard dejected Russian prisoners after the Battle of Łódź. Poor leadership, training, and equipment meant that many thousands of Russian soldiers were taken prisoner in the early battles of the war.

from the south and even the reluctant Rennenkampf returned from the east. The leading German forces seemed trapped, but they managed to slip away over the icy roads before the Russians could close in.

The Battle of Łódź had ended in stalemate, but it had significant consequences. The Russian high command ordered a withdrawal to the Vistula River. Meanwhile Ludendorff argued that Łódź was a great victory, stopping the Russian invasion of Germany before it began. With more troops from the Western Front, he said, he could force a Russian collapse. Unconvinced, Falkenhayn sent him only eight divisions, some 100,000 men.

The bolstered German forces captured Łódź on December 6. The decisive victory the Germans sought on the Eastern Front, however, was still nowhere in sight.

Life in
POLAND

In 1914 Poland was divided between the Russians, Austrians, and Germans, but the Poles wanted independence.

The war was particularly difficult for the Poles. The region that comprises today's Poland saw some of the fiercest and most destructive fighting on the Eastern Front. In 1914 alone all the fighting associated with the battles of Zamosc-Komarów and Łódź, and the siege of Przemysl took place on Polish soil.

Poland had last existed as an independent state late in the 18th century, when war had wiped the country off the map. Prussia – later Germany – Austria, and Russia divided Polish territory among themselves. When war broke out in 1914, each of these states had a significant number of Polish citizens. Poles from Austria and Germany, drafted into the army, found themselves ordered to shoot at Poles serving in the Russian forces. Not all Polish troops were draftees, however: Each partitioning power had its share of Polish supporters. Volunteers formed a Polish Legion to serve with the Austrian army against the Russians, for example.

Nationalist dreams

Despite being subject peoples, many Poles were not particularly interested in change. At the beginning of the war few of them believed that the conflict would change their homeland's status. Most were more concerned with surviving the war and protecting their property. A Pole from Galicia – the Polish region of the Austro-Hungarian Empire – complained that some villagers supported the war because they expected to sell grain to the Austrian army at higher prices than in peacetime.

Other Poles, however, saw the war as a chance to regain their national independence. Before the fighting had even begun, Polish intellectuals and students joined paramilitary groups to fight for Poland's freedom. Having had their dreams of liberation dashed for decades by Germany, Russia, and Austria, these Poles now looked forward to being able to take revenge for failed uprisings and former persecutions. Only time would tell if their expectations would be fulfilled.

German soldiers examine goods sold by Jewish market traders in a Polish town captured from the Russians. The Jews of Poland and western Russia were persecuted by the Russians during the war – although never as badly as they were later by the Nazis – supposedly because they secretly supported Germany.

The Battle of MASURIAN LAKES

Fought in incredibly fierce conditions in East Prussia, the so-called "Winter Battle" brought the German attackers thousands of prisoners but only a minor victory.

Generalleutnant Ludendorff

Generalfeldmarschall v. Hindenburg mit seinem Stabe

Generalfeldmarschall v. Hindenburg

Hindenburg, Ludendorff, and their staff pose for a photographer on the steps of German headquarters.

OPPOSING FORCES	German: 150,000	Russian: 150,000
COMMANDERS	Tenth Army: Eichorn; Eighth Army: Below	Tenth Army: Sievers
LOCATION	The eastern region of East Prussia into Russian Poland	
DURATION	February 7 – 21, 1915	
OUTCOME	German armies occupy some Russian territory.	
CASUALTIES	German: approx. 4,500	Russian: 56,000

For four months after their glorious victory at Tannenberg the German commanders Hindenburg and Ludendorff had insisted that they could win the war in the east. They believed that they had pushed the Russian army to the verge of collapse. Now they believed that they only needed additional troops and one more great effort to finish it off.

In December 1914 Ludendorff tried to make the breakthrough, with support from troops who had arrived from the battle of Łódź. But the German assault on the Russian lines in central Poland brought only another stalemate; Hindenburg and Ludendorff had lost 100,000 men, including many of the new troops. The opposing forces dug into trenches for the winter.

Meanwhile, in Silesia to the south the Austrians had pushed the Russians back into the Carpathian Mountains along the San River but could not deal a decisive blow. Winter now became the common enemy. Both sides froze in the mountains.

A combined attack

The beginning of 1915 brought the Germans new grounds for optimism. Eager to compensate for their lack of victories on the Western Front, the German high command sent Hindenburg four new army corps. It was his chance to fulfill his promise of a knockout blow to Russia through a combined German-Austrian offensive.

Hindenburg's allies, however, failed to deliver. On January 23, 1915, the Austrians launched their assault in the Carpathians, planning to break through and relieve the besieged fortress at Przemysl. The weather turned the attack into a complete disaster. Whole units froze to death, supplies could not be moved, and rifles had to be thawed out before they could be fired. The offensive gained almost no ground.

Ludendorff's plan

In the north, meanwhile, Ludendorff prepared to attack the Russian Tenth Army at the Masurian Lakes in East Prussia. He hoped ultimately to drive the Russians from Poland altogether. This was the second battle in the marshy, waterlogged

Left: The last czar, Nicholas II, displays a religious icon to his troops.

Below: German gunners in their hideout.

COMMANDERS

Hermann von Eichhorn 1848–1918 German general

Initially intended to command a unit against France, Eichorn was seriously injured in a riding accident on the eve of the war. Ready for duty in 1915, he was assigned to head the newly formed Tenth Army in East Prussia. For his service on the Eastern Front Eichorn was awarded a medal for merit in 1915. Two years later he was promoted to the rank of field marshal.

In 1918 Eichorn became commander of a new army group in the Ukraine. He attempted to exploit the region's rich grain resources for the German war effort but was ultimately unsuccessful. In July 1918 he was assassinated in Kiev by a young radical.

A German regiment prepares for action.

EYEWITNESS

The German General Hindenburg later recalled the horrors of battle in winter:

66 The name [of the Battle of Masurian Lakes] charms like an icy wind or the silence of death. As men look back on the course of this battle they will only stand and ask themselves, "Have earthly beings really done these things or is it all but a fable or a phantom? Are not these marches in the winter nights, that camp in the icy snowstorm and that last phase of the battle in the forest of Augustovo so terrible for the enemy but the creation of an inspired human fancy?" 99

region. The first battle had been fought there after Tannenberg, as the Germans had annihilated Rennenkampf's Russian army and driven it from East Prussia.

The force of winter

From the start the winter weather nearly sabotaged Ludendorff's plan to encircle the Russians. A blinding snowstorm raged across the front, delaying the German advance. Thick snow piled up as tall as the men themselves. Sometimes it took up to ten horses to move the artillery guns. And the frozen infantry crawled forward at a snail's pace.

Despite the conditions the German Eighth Army struck on February 7, driving back the southern wing of the Russian army. Hampered by poor communications – a constant problem – the Russian high command misjudged Ludendorff's plans. They assumed that his main target was nearby cities rather than the Tenth Army itself. By the time they realized their error

around a week after the first attack, two of their army's three corps were already being forced to retreat through the Augustovo Forest.

While these corps managed to escape, the remaining corps was not so lucky. By February 16 the Germans had encircled the forest. The Russians were trapped. Over the next five days Ludendorff's armies closed the circle. On February 21 some 12,000 Russian troops surrendered. This brought the total of Tenth Army losses alone up to 56,000.

Minimal gains

Ludendorff's victory, spectacular though it was, gained little apart from a small advance into Russian territory. Even that could not last long. Over the next few weeks a series of less spectacular attacks by both sides balanced the score. By early March the Germans had retreated back to the East Prussian border.

alternatives

What if the German had concentrated their efforts on the Eastern Front in early 1915? Could they have knocked Russia out of the war, as Hindenburg and Ludendorff insisted? The answer is probably not. Even if the Germans managed to hold off the Allies in the west, winning a decisive victory over the Russians would not have been easy. The further the Germans attacked into the expanses of Russia, the more likely that their supply lines would become overextended. If anything the Germans might have done Nicholas II a favor had they struck into Russian territory. A defensive war to repel the invader might well have united the Russian people around their czar.

The good soldier Švejk

"Švejk... I'll have you shot... Are you really such a half-wit?"

"Humbly report, sir, I am."

Jaroslav Hašek's story *The Good Soldier Švejk*, published in 1923, is a classic antiwar novel that appeared after World War I. Josef Švejk, a Czech soldier in the Austrian army, overcomes the authorities who run the war by pretending to be stupid. Thrown in an asylum, arrested as a spy, he emerges unscathed time after time and safely survives the entire war.

Švejk was something of a national stereotype. The Czechs themselves earned a reputation among their Austrian governors as passive resistors, and Czech soldiers as uncooperative and unreliable.

WHERE TO FIND...

Fortresses: 4:28
Radio: 6:15
Artillery: 3:14
Prisoners of War: 7:100
Nicholas II: 1:44

Polish
POLITICAL ACTIVISM

The war gave Polish nationalists a chance to assert their independence but they had to choose whether Germany, Austria, or Russia would help them most.

Crowds gather in a street in the Polish town of Łódź. In 1914 Łódź was part of the Russian Empire.

Far right: Polish refugees carry all their family possessions on carts after they have been displaced from their homes by the war.

Poland did not exist as an independent country in 1914. The Polish people, however, had their own language and national identity. They also had a long and proud history. But before World War I the last time an independent Polish state had existed was in the 18th century. After that Poland had been partitioned, or divided up, by Prussia, Austria, and Russia.

In 1914 different parts of the former Polish lands still belonged to the Russian, Austrian, and German empires, with the largest area belonging to imperial Russia. Now the three empires had gone to war with each other. They would all want loyal support from the Poles. Perhaps, Polish nationalists thought, they could turn the situation to their advantage and trade this support for their independence.

Austria, or Germany, or Russia?

Polish nationalists had been active within Austria and Russia before the war. Germany had few Polish friends because most Poles thought the Germans wanted more rather than less control of Poland's western provinces. Polish nationalists developed two principal viewpoints, one pro-Russian, the other pro-Austrian.

Roman Dmowski was the leader of the pro-Russian camp. Dmowski argued that the greatest threat to the Polish people were the Germans. In response he called for a close association with Russia as the only means of national survival.

At the beginning of the war Dmowski did everything in his power to get the Russians to commit themselves to the unification of the Polish lands. The Russians made vague promises, but they ignored Polish requests to have more say in their own government.

Józef Piłsudski had a different approach. In 1914 Piłsudski correctly predicted the outcome of the war. He said that Germany

politics

Russian promises

On August 14, 1914, the commander in chief of the Russian armed forces, the Grand Duke Nicholas issued the following manifesto to the Polish people:

"Poles! The hour has struck when the dreams of your fathers and forefathers can come true. A century and a half ago, the living body of Poland was torn in pieces; but her soul did not die. It was kept alive by a hope for the resurrection of the Polish nation and for its fraternal union with Great Russia.

The Russian Army brings you the blessed news of that union. May the frontiers that cut across the Polish nation be erased. May the Polish nation be joined in one under the scepter of the Russian Emperor. Under that scepter Poland will be reborn, free in her own faith, language, and self-rule."

Did the Russians mean what they said? Some Poles doubted it. They noticed that the posters the Russians issued to publicize the promise had the Polish flag printed upside-down.

Roman Dmowski 1864–1939
Polish politician
Roman Dmowski was one of the founders of modern Polish nationalism.

Dmowski argued that only Poles could be the foundation for the Polish state. He claimed that Poland's large Jewish population could not be blended in. Anti-Semitism was a central plank of Dmowski's political ideas.

Dmowski was a member of the Russian parliament before the war. During the war he moved to the West to try to get Britain and France to support Polish independence.

Dmowski was a negotiator for Poland at the Paris Peace Conference in 1919. He rarely held political positions in Poland after that, but his ideas remained important in Polish national life.

after all three partitioning states were defeated.

In 1914 Piłsudski took command of a Polish unit in the Austrian army. But although he believed that Russia was the greatest obstacle to Polish freedom, he was not loyal to the Hapsburg monarchy he served. He did not share the Austrians' vision of Poland's future – they wanted to make Poland part of a new Austrian-Hungarian-Polish state. The

and Austria would beat Russia but would be beaten in turn by the Western Powers. Piłsudski thought that a Polish military force would then be the decisive factor

determined Piłsudski was prepared to cooperate with the Austrians only for as long as it brought him nearer to his ultimate goal: Polish independence.

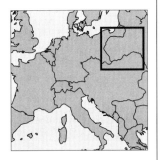

The GORLICE–TARNOW OFFENSIVE

A conclusive victory in the east still eluded the Central Powers, but the spring of 1915 heralded an assault in Galicia that would strain the Russians almost to breaking point.

German troops prepare to continue the advance against the retreating Russians during the battles in Galicia.

FactFile

OPPOSING FORCES (May 2, 1915)	German: 126,000 Austrian: 90,000	Russian: 219,000
COMMANDERS	German: Eleventh Army: Mackensen; Austrian: Fourth Army: Archduke Josef Ferdinand	Third Army: Dimitriev; Southwest Army Group: Ivanov
LOCATION	28-mile front between the towns of Gorlice and Tarnow in Austrian Galicia	
DURATION	May 2 – June 27, 1915	
OUTCOME	Russian threat to Hungary repelled. Central Powers push Russian armies out of Austrian Galicia.	
CASUALTIES	German: 90,000	Russian (including Narew offensive): 1,410,000; 976,000 prisoners

By May 1915 the war in the east was nine months old. Despite the promises of the German high command the Central Powers had not yet achieved a decisive victory.

The Russians – despite great losses – had refused to give up. The German advance had been halted in Poland and East Prussia. To the south the Russians had driven the Austrians from Galicia and now threatened to invade Hungary.

But with the spring weather came new danger. The Central Powers planned an offensive between the Galician towns of Gorlice and Tarnow.

Left: Russian soldiers in their trenches.

White arrows show the Central Powers' attacks into Russia in 1915.

The offensive coincided with a change in German strategy. In the first months of year the military leadership in Berlin had realized that it was fruitless to try to break the stalemate of the trenches on the Western Front. Instead they decided to crush Russia once and for all by concentrating the energies of the German army on the Eastern Front.

The attack begins

The Central Powers decided to attack in spring, when the harsh winter was over. It was warmer, and, after the thaw, the roads were passable again. The Austro-German forces planned to strike along the 28-mile front between Gorlice and Tarnow. They wanted to push the Russians back a short way, preferably to the San River.

On May 2 German artillery opened the attack with a four-hour barrage, pulverizing the Russian Third Army, which held that part of the front. Any Russians who survived the shells fled back into open country with the Germans in hot pursuit. In just 12 days the forces of the Central Powers advanced 80 miles. Their rapid progress put them in a strong position, for they now threatened the flanks and rear of other Russian units.

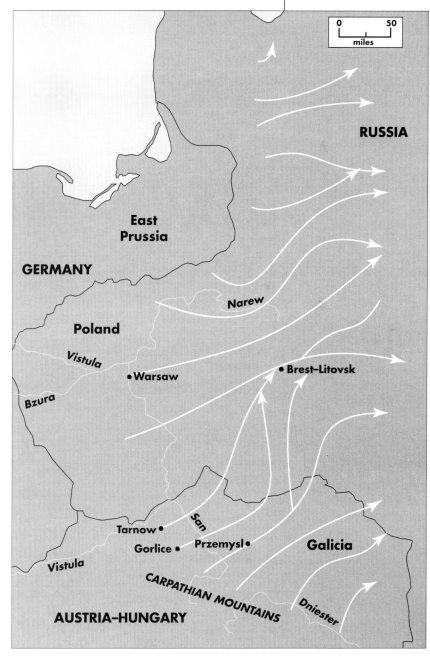

A lone German sentry looks out from his trench during the campaign in Galicia.

**Nikolai Ludovich Ivanov
1851–1919
Russian general**

Popular with the Russian army's peasant recruits, Ivanov enjoyed the reputation of an expert on modern warfare. His long career of service included a corps command in the Russo-Japanese War from 1904 to 1905 and a stint as the head of the Kiev Military District. As commander of the Southwest Army Group, he observed firsthand the effectiveness of German infantry–artillery cooperation during the Gorlice–Tarnow offensive.

Replaced by Brusilov in early 1916, he was made advisor to the czar. Ivanov remained loyal to Nicholas II during the Russian Revolution, taking command of a counter-revolutionary unit on the Don River in October 1918. He died of typhus in January 1919.

The retreating Russians faced disaster. A shortage of supplies made their situation even more desperate. The Third Army quickly ran out of artillery shells. General Nikolai Ivanov, commanding the Southwest Army Group, frantically pleaded for more. But, like other European armies, the Russians had severely underestimated the number of shells they would need to fight the war. Stavka – the Russian army headquarters – could send the Third Army barely half of what they asked for. The factories had not even produced the rest.

The ammunition that did exist could often not be delivered to the front due to the poor state of the Russian railroads. Worse still, Stavka insisted on stockpiling shells in outdated fortresses. Before the war reformers had argued that this was foolish; the officers in charge had ignored them. Now the desperately needed shells and guns were locked up miles away from the fighting.

The advance gathers pace

Despite his lack of supplies, the commander of the Third Army, General Dimitriev, tried to counterattack. But fresh German troops, thrown against his positions, only added to his growing losses. Stavka, how-

Bells removed from a Russian town, probably for melting down, stand in the garden of a Russian monastery.

ever, was determined not to yield any more ground to the enemy and refused to allow the Third Army to withdraw. Resistance could not last: On May 10 Stavka ordered Dimitriev to fall back to the San River.

There was no reason to think the Germans and Austrians could be stopped there; the Russians had no time to prepare any defensive positions. The German forces surged forward. By May 19 they had pushed the Russians across the San. Now they pressed south toward the Russian-held fortress of Przemysl. Again the Russians put up fierce resistance, particularly against the Austrians. The battered Austrians needed help from the Germans to hold their lines. Still the Central Powers advanced steadily. By June 3 they had captured Przemysl.

For the Russians there was no help in sight. Although the Italians had just entered the war against the Central Powers, they were not yet a strong enough threat to force the Austrians to divert

An aerial photograph shows clouds of poison gas drifting toward the Russian lines.

troops from Galicia to face them. Russia's western allies were bogged down in France and Belgium. The Russian armies had no option but retreat. Over the course of June Ivanov's forces fell back across the next major river, the Dniester. The Central Powers had retaken Galicia and driven the Russians back into their own territory.

A vital victory

The Central Powers' spring offensive had important repercussions. Morale in Austria had been low after the winter stalemate in the Carpathians and Italy's entry into the war on the side of the Allies. Now this old news was offset by press reports from Galicia. The region's oil fields were regained and put back into production. Throughout the empire religious services celebrated the recapture of Przemysl and Lemberg (Lvov), the Galician capital.

The victory also inspired Bulgaria to consider joining the Central Powers, while Romania hesitated to come into the war alongside Russia and her allies. Things were going well for the Central Powers. The Russians would not have time to regroup before the Germans struck again to the north with equally devastating consequences for the forces of Czar Nicholas II.

EYEWITNESS

A Russian officer described his army's disastrous supply shortages to the French ambassador to Petrograd, Maurice Paleologue:

❝ We are not producing more than 24,000 shells a day. It's a pittance for so vast a front! But our shortage of rifles alarms me far more. Just think! In several infantry regiments that have taken part in the recent battles at least one third of the men had no rifle. These poor devils had to wait patiently under a shower of shrapnel until their comrades fell before their eyes and they could pick up their arms … ❞

A German officer inspects dead Russians after a German gas attack.

tactics

Hurricane of fire

A number of German troops fighting in the Gorlice–Tarnow offensive had already seen action on the Western Front. There they had learned several tactical lessons. They appreciated the importance of observation and the necessity of coordinating the actions of infantry and artillery. The balance struck between these two arms of the German army, first used in the opening days of the offensive, resulted in a method of attack described by Russian soldiers as a "hurricane of fire."

First, the Germans used heavy artillery to smash the first line of Russian trenches. Just as the bombardment let up, an infantry assault struck. As the Germans reaimed their guns to fire at the Russian artillery, waves of foot-soldiers pushed forward to capture what remained of the enemy line. Then they moved their big guns forward, and the whole process was repeated against the next Russian positions.

After this offensive the Russians attempted to mimic these tactics. But the results were disappointing. Inaccurate heavy artillery bombardment churned up the ground so badly that it became nearly impossible for the infantry to advance. And because they needed to concentrate guns and soldiers in order to attack, the Russians lost the element of surprise.

WHERE TO FIND...

Artillery: 3:14
Supply Lines: 2:76
Siege of Przemysl: 6:30
Italy Enters the War: 3:64
Poison Gas: 3:55

Far right: Tomáš Masaryk, Czech nationalist leader.

Workers test artillery at a Czech Skoda arms factory. Czech weapons and troops served in the Austrian army during World War I.

Czech
POLITICAL ACTIVISM

The coming of war provided an opportunity for Czech nationalists to press for independence. But their campaign would be long and difficult.

In common with other ethnic groups living in Austria-Hungary, the Czechs were recruited into the Austro-Hungarian army. Most fought on the Eastern Front. But many disliked having to fight the Russians who, like them, were Slavs.

Most Czechs were equally unhappy with living under Austro-Hungarian rule. Some wanted to join Russia in a pan-Slav empire bringing together all the Slavic peoples. Others dreamed of creating a kingdom with the neighboring Slovaks, with a

Russian grand duke on the throne. They hoped that Russian troops would soon be marching into the Czech capital of Prague.

In August 1914 a Russian victory looked unlikely. The most Czech nationalists hoped for was that Austria-Hungary might become a federation of equal states. This form of government would give them the same rights as the other ethnic groups in the empire. With this hope most Czech political parties pledged their allegiance to the Austrian war effort. Only one party suggested that the Czechs should take the chance to break Austro-Hungarian rule.

A determined campaigner

One of the Czech politicians who opposed the Austrians was Tomáš Masaryk. But he was also against closer ties with Russia. Masaryk believed that being under the oppressive control of the czar was little better than living under the Hapsburgs. Instead he wanted a completely independent state for the Czechs and Slovaks.

Masaryk turned toward the western Allies. In December 1914 he fled Prague and went to Geneva, in Switzerland. In March 1915 he moved to London, which he considered the political center of the Allies. He began a determined campaign to make Czechoslovak independence an international issue and enlist Allied sympathy and support for the cause.

While he was away from his country, Masaryk remained in constant touch with a close-knit group of nationalist activists – known as the *Maffie*, or mafia – in Prague. One of the group's members, Edvard Beneš, was particularly energetic in fighting for independence. In 1915 Beneš also left Prague and went to Paris. Together

with Masaryk he formed the Czechoslovak National Council to coordinate the campaign. While Masaryk played an ambassadorial role, negotiating with the Allied governments, Beneš planned the political direction of the movement.

They had a difficult road ahead. In the first two years of the war the western Allies had shown no intention of breaking up Austria-Hungary. They believed that the empire ensured stability in eastern Europe. The British and the French viewed the Czechoslovak cause as an internal Austrian problem, just as they saw Polish independence as a matter of Russian domestic politics. All Masaryk and Beneš could do was vigorously promote the Czechoslovak cause. They could only hope that the Allies would soon begin to listen.

WAR PROFILES

Tomáš Masaryk 1850–1937
Czech politician
Called the "liberator" and "founder" of his country, Tomáš Masaryk became the first president of Czechoslovakia when the state was created after the collapse of Austria-Hungary in 1918.

At the start of the war Masaryk's greatest fear was a resurgence of Germany's military power, which he considered to be the principal threat to European peace. But he believed an era of democracy would follow an Allied victory.

Married to an American woman and western in his outlook, Masaryk turned toward Britain and France rather than Russia in his wartime campaign for an independent Czechoslovak state.

He remained president until his resignation in 1935. He died two years later.

The Fall of
POLAND

Germany overran Poland and captured many vital Russian supplies. Still, however, they could not achieve a truly decisive defeat of the Russian armies.

Russians lie dead on the battlefield, having been caught by a heavy German bombardment during the German advance in the northern sector of the front in 1915.

Defeat in the Battle of Gorlice-Tarnow forced the Russian army out of the Austrian province of Galicia. Now Russian-held Poland was a dangerously isolated bulge, or salient. The enemy threatened it not just from the front but on the flanks. To the north the Germans occupied East Prussia; to the south lay the Austrian and German forces in Galicia. Both sides saw that the Russians would probably have to retreat from their exposed position. For the Central Powers, however, inflicting a telling defeat on the enemy was far from straightforward.

Divisions in the German command

The German generals Hindenburg and Ludendorff – the heroes of 1914 who commanded the northern part of the front – called for an attack to the north. German forces would swing around far behind the Russian forces within the salient and cut

German soldiers examine one of the guns of the Russian fortress of Kovno. Kovno was captured by the German Tenth Army on August 18, 1915. The gun shown is one of a number made for the Russians by their former enemies, the Japanese.

them off. It would be a repeat of the tactics that had won the Battle of Tannenberg, but on an even bigger scale.

Focusing on France

Back in Germany, however, the grand plan seemed less tempting. The Kaiser and General Erich von Falkenhayn, his overall commander, believed that they should concentrate their efforts on the Western Front. A drive so far into Russia, they argued, would not bring a decisive victory. The enemy could retreat indefinitely into the vast hinterland of their country.

Instead, Falkenhayn suggested a simpler plan to trap the Russians. The Central Powers would launch a three-pronged attack into Poland: north from Galicia; southeast across the Narew River toward the Polish capital, Warsaw; and south from East Prussia.

FactFile

OPPOSING FORCES	German and Austrian: unknown	Russia: unknown
COMMANDERS	German: Ninth Army: Prince Leopold; Tenth Army: Eichorn; Eleventh Army: Mackensen; Twelfth Army: Gallwitz; Austrian: Fourth Army: Archduke Josef Ferdinand	Regional commander: Alexeiev; First Army: Litvinov; Third Army: Lesh; Fourth Army: Evert; Fifth Army: Plehve; Twelfth Army: Churin
LOCATION	(Galicia) 90-mile front between the Bug and Vistula Rivers; (Narew) 25-mile front between Polish towns of Przasnysz and Ciechanowska; (Courland) 160-mile front from the Baltic Sea to the west of Kovno	
DURATION	June 29 – September 19, 1915	
OUTCOME	Russians forced to evacuate Russian Poland, Lithuania, and parts of Latvia and Belarus.	
CASUALTIES	German and Austrian: unknown	Russian (incl. Gorlice-Tarnow and the Great Retreat): 1,210,000 dead/wounded; 1,042,200 prisoners

Far right: Mikhail Alexeiev, regional commander on the Russian western front in 1915.

A long column of Russian prisoners trudging into German captivity along a street in Vilnius. Vilnius was captured by the Germans in the September fighting. But most of the Russian defenders in the area avoided a German attempt to surround them and retreated.

EYEWITNESS

After facing the heavy firepower the Germans now deployed on the Eastern Front, a Russian corps commander wrote to a fellow officer about the devastating effects of German tactics and the Russian inability to cope with them:

❝ The Germans plow up the battlefields with a hail of metal and level our trenches and fortifications, the fire often burying the defenders of the trenches in them. The Germans expend metal, we expend life. They go forward and, encouraged by their success, take risks, whereas we only beat them off by paying with heavy losses and our blood, and are retreating. This has a very unfavorable influence on the spirit of all. ❞

The Russian high command faced a dilemma. They could easily see the danger of their armies' exposed positions, but for various reasons they could not withdraw from Poland without a fight. For one thing, a series of great fortresses guarded the region. Not only were they planned as the ultimate defense against an invader; they were also vital supply bases. Combined, they held more than 9,000 artillery pieces and 100 million rounds of ammunition. The Russian commanders could only hope that the experience of the Western Front – where German guns neutralized the fortresses of Belgium and France – would not be repeated.

The advance begins

The offensive began in the south on July 12 but moved slowly. The troops were weary and the railroads inadequate. The Austrians, in particular, were exhausted by earlier battles. The Russian line fell back but did not break. The Austrians would have to win the offensive further north instead.

In central Poland Germany's General Max von Gallwitz began his march on Warsaw with a devastatingly effective artillery bombardment. It seemed likely that his men would soon be in the Polish capital.

As he advanced to the Narew River, however, Russian resistance stiffened.

It was only a temporary respite for the desperate defenders. Further north other German units had besieged the fortress of Kovno and struck deep into Latvia. Along the way they had captured Szawli – also called Schaulen, an important leather-making town. The town's fall had important consequences. The invaders seized many animal hides, depriving the Russians of a vital supply of boots for their footsore and exhausted armies.

Despite their resistance on the Narew, the Russians could now see only one way to save their armies in Poland: They would have to retreat.

THE COMMANDERS

Mikhail Vasilevich Alexeiev 1857–1918
Russian officer
Beginning the war as chief of staff of the southwest front, Alexeiev became one of the most important officers in the Russian army. After the czar took personal command of the army in August 1915, Alexeiev was his chief of staff. A talented organizer and planner, he overhauled Stavka, the army headquarters, and stabilized the front, enabling the Russian army to attack in 1916.

After the February Revolution Alexeiev was briefly supreme commander of the Russian army. Once the Bolsheviks came to power, Alexeiev helped to raise the anti-Bolshevik Volunteer Army. He died in October 1918.

politics

Austrian-German tensions

Even the Central Powers' great victories over Russia in 1915 could not reduce the growing tensions between the Austrian and German generals. From the outset of war the Austrians had been convinced that the Germans saw the Eastern Front as only secondary to the war in the west; for their part the Germans doubted the fighting abilities of the Austrian army. When the Germans did, indeed, prove more successful at fighting the Russians, they began to treat their allies as junior partners, which Austrian officers thoroughly resented.

Political misunderstandings did nothing to smooth things out. The Austrians assumed that the Polish territories seized from Russia in 1915 would become part of their empire. The German high command had other ideas. By 1917 such disagreements had convinced the Austrians that the only way forward was to open peace negotiations with Russia, ideally alongside Germany but, if necessary, alone.

The RUSSIAN GREAT RETREAT

As the Russians withdrew before the advance of the Central Powers, their retreat turned into a disorderly race for safety.

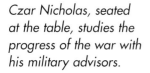

Czar Nicholas, seated at the table, studies the progress of the war with his military advisors.

The German advances of spring 1915 – into Poland and Latvia further north – had pushed the Russians to their limit. In July Stavka – the Russian high command – bowed to the inevitable and ordered a general retreat. It would last until the end of September as the Central Powers made dramatic gains; in places they advanced a massive 300 miles.

On July 22 the Russians facing General Max von Gallwitz on the Narew River began to withdraw to the east. Those opposing General August von Mackensen at Lublin and Cholm, meanwhile, moved to the north. At the beginning of August the Russians fell back again. This time they did not stop until the end of September.

The Russians suffer

Although what became known as the "Great Retreat" started in an orderly way, the pullback eastward quickly degenerated into chaos. Such was the rush that at one point Stavka completely lost control of the army. Groups of soldiers fell back with no orders; there was no coordination of the different bodies of men.

It was not only the troops who were retreating. Civilian refugees, fleeing the advancing enemy, clogged the army's retreat routes. Forced from their homes, whole families had taken to the road, their belongings piled onto a cart or carried in sacks. Military units pushed the refugees from the roads to get by.

The sense of panic had spread far from the front. In Petrograd residents looked on anxiously as the government made preparations to move Russia's state archives and

gold reserves out of the capital for safety in case the Germans came.

Some blame for the panic lay with the Russian army's commander in chief, Grand Duke Nikolai Nikolaevich, uncle of the czar. He had made no plans for the retreat. As Stavka's orders became more frantic, he panicked so much that his wife feared he would have a nervous breakdown. The grand duke's nephew, Czar Nicholas, decided to take over supreme command of the Russian armed forces.

EYEWITNESS

A Russian general reported how discipline broke down among the armies during the Great Retreat:

66 The Ministry of the Interior has received information about extraordinary plundering in the rear of the army, particularly on the [Russian] Western Front. Instances are cited of disobedience to officers, including one ending with murder in Baranovichi. Prince Shcherbatov, Minister of the Interior, personally observed on September 16 in Orsha a spectacle of unheard-of disorderliness among a crowd of two and a half thousand recuperated wounded. On the railroads an increasing number of soldiers lack documents. These deserters are stirring up the people with imaginary stories slandering the commanding staff. 99

German troopers advance to Warsaw, the capital of Poland.

A bridge destroyed by retreating Russians. Scorched earth tactics aimed to destroy anything that might be of use to the enemy.

Scorched earth

The Russian high command's decision to destroy anything that might be of use to the advancing Central Powers enraged the inhabitants of the region. Attempting to imitate the retreat of the Russian armies before Napoleon in 1812, Stavka ordered

withdrawing units to burn dwellings, destroy crops, cut down trees, and force thousands of people to evacuate. Even Russian peasant soldiers were appalled by the carnage and the injustice of this action. Whereas officials showed no mercy to the local peasants, wealthy landowners could usually bribe soldiers to leave their property alone. Senior officers transported their furniture and even their pets while helpless peasants headed eastward with nothing.

The Germans understood the Russian methods, but they marveled at the inconsistency of the effort. In some areas the destruction was complete; in others there was barely any damage at all. As one German officer later wrote: "The Russian destructions were in many ways an advantage for us. … Although [Brest-Litovsk, for example,] was burned down, we were able to find quarters there, while the 80,000 inhabitants for whom we should have had to provide were not there."

The Russian army also earned the lasting enmity of the Polish peasantry. Before the withdrawal Polish villagers maintained relatively cordial relations with the Russians. Now cooperation ceased, and there were even cases of resistance. The Great Retreat convinced Polish peasants that the Russians were not their friends. And as a result the Russians would find little support for their future struggles in this region.

Russian prisoners who have not escaped in the Great Retreat trudge into captivity.

As the Russians retreated, so the advancing enemy filled the vacuum. On August 4 the Germans entered the Polish capital, Warsaw. Fifteen days later the fortress of Novo-Georgievsk – with stores of 1,600 artillery pieces and nearly one million shells – surrendered. Further north, meanwhile, Eichorn's Tenth Army made easy progress into Lithuania, capturing the province's capital, Vilnius. Relief eventually came for the Russians. On September 18 the German high command halted the campaign for the winter.

The Central Powers' armies lay deep in Russian territory. The front stretched 600 miles from the Gulf of Riga in the north through the Pripet Marshes to the Romanian border in the south. The two sides dug into trenches. Despite the efforts of Russian artillery bombardments to achieve a breakthrough, the stalemate would continue until the following summer.

The Russian withdrawal had political as well as military consequences. At home the czar's political opponents were now in a stronger position. More seriously, however, Nicholas himself was at the front rather than in Petrograd. In his absence Russian politics fell into incapable hands – with drastic consequences.

EYEWITNESS

The retreat brought terrible suffering to millions of Russian civilians. One medical orderly remembered the desperate scene when guards allowed refugees to come near the army's field kitchens:

66 Men tore basins of food from each others' hands ... [while] women with starving children at their breasts hastily crammed pieces of gray stewed pork into their mouths and trampled others underfoot. 99

WHERE TO FIND...

Mackensen: 3:105
Nicholas II: 1:44
**Two Emperors'
 Manifesto: 6:**76

The BRUSILOV OFFENSIVE

Russia's most successful military operation of the war pushed the Austrian forces back along a wide front, but both Russia and Austria were left weaker than when the battle began.

At the start of 1916 the Russian army appeared to be on its last legs. The defeats of 1915 had driven it from Poland at a cost of two million soldiers killed, wounded, or taken prisoner. The blow to Russian prestige prompted unrest at home. In several cities demonstrations openly criticized the government and military authorities. Yet, remarkably, the new year would see the Russian army's most effective attacks of the war.

Russia's army leaders quickly responded to the crisis with a thorough reorganization. The influential commander in chief, General Mikhail Alexeiev, introduced more central planning. He wanted military

Right: The white arrows on the map show the Russian offensive which took place in June 1916. An intended supporting attack by General Evert northwest toward Kovel failed to materialize.

Map labels:
Pripet Marshes • Kovel • RUSSIA • Lutsk • Front Line Mid-July 1916 • Front Line June 4 1916 • Lvov • Dniester • AUSTRIA-HUNGARY • Prut • Czernowitz

0 — 20 miles

strategy coordinated not only among the Russian armies but with the entire Allied war effort. Many Russian officers began to think about new ways to fight a trench war. Some of them came up with answers.

FactFile

OPPOSING FORCES	German and Austrian: 500,000	Russian: 600,000
COMMANDERS	Front commander: Linsingen	C o S: Alexeiev; commander: Brusilov
LOCATION	200-mile front south of the Pripet Marshes to the Romanian frontier	
DURATION	June 4 – October 10, 1916	
OUTCOME	Russians recapture Bukovina and seize portions of Austrian Galicia.	
CASUALTIES	German and Austrian: 370,000 dead/ wounded	Russian: more than 200,000 dead/ wounded

The most pressing problem was how to break through the enemy lines. Like the armies on the Western Front, the Russians found a well-dug-in enemy almost impossible to overcome. The problem was confirmed in March. Intending to relieve their French allies – then besieged in the fortress of Verdun on the Western Front – the Russians had launched an offensive in the northern part of the line, at Lake Naroch. Despite ample manpower and plenty of shells, the attack had achieved nothing but more casualties.

In June the Russians again answered the call of an ally in need. This time it was the Italians, who were fiercely resisting an Austrian attack in the Alps, the mountain range that divided the two countries. The Russians launched an offensive against the Germans north of the Pripet River; but the commander, General Alexei Evert, was pessimistic that he would achieve much. Further south, however, General Alexei Brusilov declared that he, too, would attack, and that he would get results.

A tactical breakthrough

Brusilov's confidence came from his decision to try a new approach from the usual Russian tactics. Instead of using artillery to try to pound the enemy into submission, he ordered his four armies to strike together without a long preparatory bombardment. Over the course of the war both sides had gotten so used to weathering artillery barrages that all they sometimes achieved was

Russian troops in position in No Man's Land, ready to breach the enemy barbed wire and begin their attack.

Russian industry

People used to believe that Russian industry during World War I was primitive and poorly developed, incapable of meeting the material needs of modern warfare, and that this was why the Germans crushed the Russians. This was only partly true.

Like other countries before 1914, the Russians had only planned for a short war. The high command (Stavka) believed that building up a reserve stock of guns and shells would be sufficient for the army, rather than planning for increased production. When it became clear that the conflict would drag on, the Russian high command attempted to buy arms from Britain and America. But there were considerable delays and the prices charged to the Russians were prohibitively high. The Russians received precious little equipment and arms in 1915 when they needed it most. The whole affair inspired little trust in foreign suppliers.

Yet the Russians also hurt themselves by failing to expand their own industry quickly and efficiently. Supply officers did not trust reports coming in from the front about the rate of shell use. They thought that fighting units were just trying to hoard supplies. When it became clear that the shortage was real, rivalries between government agencies, and distrust between the government and industrialists, slowed production once more.

When the Russians finally got organized, however, industry proved to be more than adequate for the armed forces' extensive requirements. During 1916 Russian factories churned out all sorts of army equipment, from field telephones to automobiles. By 1917 the production of shells and guns was close to meeting, if it had not already met, the army's ideal supply figures.

But this increased production had widespread and ominous repercussions. An enormous strain was put on the domestic front in order to carry out this manufacturing program. The consequences of such discontent would be felt in the year to come, when Russian industry would increasingly struggle to cope with the enormous demand.

Brusilov struck the Austrian Fourth Army south of the Pripet Marshes on June 4, taking them completely by surprise. The enemy commander was not even with his troops: The overconfident Archduke Josef Ferdinand had gone on a hunting trip.

The Russian armies scored immediate successes. They punched a large gap in the front, forcing the Austrians to withdraw after two days. To the south of the Dniester

Below: Russian infantry in a captured German trench.

Above: All armies employed tethered balloons, flown from positions close to the front lines and defended by antiaircraft guns, to spot targets for the artillery. This one is being used by an Austro-Hungarian unit in 1917.

to signal that the enemy was about to attack. Now Brusilov hoped to achieve total surprise. He had underground bunkers built to conceal his assault troops from the enemy; he only informed even his officers of the date of the attack at the last minute. The offensive would stretch over a wide front. The enemy had no way of knowing where the main blow would fall.

THE COMMANDERS

Alexei Alexeievich Brusilov 1853–1926
Russian general

A cavalry officer with a record of service dating back to the Russo-Turkish War (1877-78), Brusilov was noted for the strict discipline of his units and for their professional conduct. In the summer of 1916 he launched the last successful offensive of the Russian Imperial Army.

After the February Revolution of 1917, Brusilov served the Provisional Government, leading the offensive ordered by War Minister Aleksandr Kerensky. After that attack's failure, Brusilov was forced into retirement. He was one of the few high-ranking Imperial Army officers who served the Bolshevik cause after 1917.

Brusilov acted as a military consultant and inspector of cavalry in 1920, when Bolshevik Russia was at war with Poland. He retired in 1924 and traveled abroad, where he was shunned by the Russian emigrant community because of his service to the Bolshevik government. He died in Moscow in 1926.

River, the Austrian Seventh Army suffered even worse. By June 12 both Austrian armies had been shattered, and Brusilov's forces had advanced 25 miles.

Brusilov kept the pressure on. By mid-June the Austrian position in Galicia lay in ruins: they had lost almost 200,000 prisoners and 700 guns to the Russian advance.

At the northern end of the front the Russians were closing in on Kovel, an important railroad junction. By now, however, German reinforcements had arrived to support the retreating Austrians. To continue the advance Brusilov would need help from General Evert's forces in the north. It would not be forthcoming.

General Brusilov at work, studying his armies' positions.

home front

War posters

The use of posters was one method employed by the Russian government to drum up support for the war effort. Images produced early in the war often showed Germans as less than human – frequently as snakes or dragons – and as un-Christian invaders who would violate the Russian Orthodox faith. As the war went on, posters were also used to persuade the Russian people to invest in war loans. This type of poster frequently depicted soldiers in combat. They suggested that by investing money the civilian would contribute to the fight against the enemy just as the soldiers were doing. Women were often shown operating machinery or serving as volunteers.

Later, posters played a valuable role in spreading the ideology of Bolshevism in the aftermath of the October

Left and below: Russian posters tried to raise money from the Russian people to help finance the war. At left the soldiers are, of course, well clothed and equipped. The poster below features the double-headed eagle, symbol of the Russian Romanov royal family.

Revolution of 1917. These portrayed peasants and workers proclaiming a government of the people. Such posters also tried to explain the new regime's goals, including the destruction of the czarist regime.

Mitteleuropa

y 1914 *Mitteleuropa*, the German word for "Central Europe," came to be understood as much more than a purely geographical term. It implied a whole program of German economic domination and near-dictatorial control of the region between Germany and Russia.

The word had first been used in the 1830s in a less ominous sense, but its meaning had changed over time. Then a number of German economists argued that a customs union between the many independent German states and the Austrian Empire would help the economy of the region grow.

The term Mitteleuropa gained a political connotation during the debates over the unification of all German lands that started in earnest in 1848. Opponents of German unity used the term to describe a reorganized Austrian state in which all peoples enjoyed equal political rights. This Mitteleuropa would act as a balance against the growing power of Prussian-dominated Germany on one side and Russia on the other.

By the first years of the 20th century the region of central Europe began to look more and more important to German economic interests. Most political leaders believed that the world was being carved up into competing economic blocs. Because of this, they argued that direct economic control of large territories was an essential target of economic policy. It was clear that the Germans understood this to mean that they should take the leading role in Mitteleuropa for themselves. The Slavic and Hungarian peoples living there would be subordinated to German

Right: The Skoda factory in what is now Czechoslovakia. Under Germany's plans for Mitteleuropa, such industries would all become part of a great German sphere of interest.

course of the war German designs on Mitteleuropa just seemed to grow. The German high command took increasingly complete control from the politicians in Germany itself and the Austro-Hungarian war effort became more dependent on the Germans also. The German generals considered all territories under their influence to be nothing more than an extended area of German rule. Even economic plans sensitive to the rights of non-Germanic peoples presumed German dominance. These views clashed with those of Austrian leaders, who saw Central Europe as a place where Hapsburg influence had to be preserved.

German schemes for Mitteleuropa also shaped the views of Britain and France, and later the United States, regarding the continued existence of Austria-Hungary. As Austria became more dependent on Germany, the Allies began to pay more attention to the Czechs, Poles, and other peoples who argued for independence from the Austrian empire.

The Western Allies seemed to be facing a crucial choice for the postwar world. This was between a policy of keeping Austria-Hungary going, under German dominance, or allowing it to collapse entirely in favor of new independent states. Gradually it became clear that the second option was the one that the Allies preferred.

economic plans and policies. In September 1914 economic dominance over central Europe was pronounced as one of Germany's war aims.

Economic control did not necessarily mean political control. Yet, over the

The KOVEL OFFENSIVE

Brusilov's advance had brought the Austrian army to the edge of disaster. But a Russian loss of nerve at the crucial moment would see the opportunity for triumph go to waste.

German officers enjoy their comfortable quarters in a commandeered house in 1916.

By June 1916 the Austrian high command was desperate: It could not stop Russia's onslaught. Russia's General Brusilov now threatened the passes through the Carpathian Mountains, passes that led straight into Hungary itself. The Austrian chief of staff, Conrad von Hötzendorf, saw disaster ahead. He wired his wife at army headquarters and warned her to get ready to evacuate.

Conrad was too pessimistic. Despite his success the frustrated Brusilov had to pause: Russian command had never intended his strike into Austrian Galicia to be the main Russian attack. That would come from General Aleksei Evert's Fourth Army, further north. But Evert showed no signs of launching his offensive. Brusilov – his supplies running low and his northern flank dangerously exposed – was beside himself with anger. In an effort to encourage Evert, Brusilov redirected some men northwest toward the railroad junction of Kovel. A German setback there might collapse the front facing Evert, making it easier for the Russians to push forward.

But Brusilov was the only Russian commander who believed in his plan. Neither Evert nor his fellow general, Aleksei Kuropatkin, thought it would work. Worse, they no longer believed that any offensive against the Germans could succeed. Since their disastrous attack at Lake Naroch in March – an attempt to divert the Germans from the Western Front – the two generals had convinced themselves that any assault would be fruitless. Now they spent June making up excuses not to adopt Brusilov's plan. Evert even argued that an attack was impossible because of the religious holidays that fell in the month.

The nervous Evert and Kuropatkin overestimated their enemy. The Germans had their own reasons to fear a combined Russian offensive. Tied down at Verdun in France and expecting a British drive on the Somme River, the Germans could not afford to send more troops to the Eastern Front. If all the Russian armies attacked – at once and in force – the defenders would struggle to hold their lines. One German officer later wrote of Kuropatkin's position in the north: "If the Russians could succeed in breaking through here, the whole of the [German] front would have to retire."

By the time Evert finally attacked on July 2, at Baranovichi, the moment had passed. To make things worse, the general had learned little from his past mistakes. He used the same tactics that had failed at Lake Naroch – massing his guns along a short front and blasting at the German

Confident after their victories, German troops in Russia have made dummies ridiculing Allied leaders, from left to right: Czar Nicholas II, Poincaré of France, Kitchener of Britain, and an Italian referred to as "Tutti Frutti."

A veteran of the Russo-Turkish and Russo-Japanese Wars, Evert earned the reputation as a cautious commander while head of the Russian Fourth Army. He remained in this position from August 1914 until the following September, when Czar Nicholas II took charge of the Russian armies himself.

Evert was then promoted to commander of the Russian Western Front. After suffering serious losses at Lake Naroch, Evert stopped believing that Russia could defeat the Germans. As a result, he did not support Brusilov's offensive in the summer of 1916. During the February Revolution Evert refused to back the czar. He was dismissed from the army in early 1917 and disappeared. It is believed that he died the following year.

positions. When the barrage stopped, the Germans simply brought their reserves into the line and repelled Evert's attempt to push through. He lost 80,000 men.

Meanwhile, Brusilov's units advanced toward Kovel. The general seemed to have forgotten his own recipe for success. In the marshy ground along the Stokhod River Brusilov returned to the all-out frontal attacks he had abandoned in June. From mid-July he hurled 250,000 troops against 115,000 Austrian and German defenders.

The Russians had more men and more shells, but the Germans had ruthlessly efficient air support. The Russian soldiers wading chest-deep in the riverside mud were sitting ducks for the machine guns of the low-flying German pilots.

The Russian advance stalled. From July to October only Brusilov's southern units made gains, pushing into the Carpathian passes. But the Russian army was exhausted. It would advance no further.

alternatives

In the summer of 1916 the German high command was gravely concerned about the ability of its armies to hold up on all fronts. Could a concerted Russian attack by both Brusilov and Evert have broken open the German defenses? Even if Evert had adapted Brusilov's tactics, it is unlikely that the Russian forces could have broken through the German defenses entirely. Brusilov's new method of attack did not allow for a great concentration of troops in order to exploit success. On the other hand, it is entirely possible that a simultaneous, all-out attack of the Russian armies could have stretched the German lines past the breaking point.

Russian troops at a field kitchen.

Breakthrough tactics

Up until the Brusilov Offensive of June 1916, the Russian army could not break through the Central Powers' lines. No matter how heavily the Russians bombarded them, the enemy knew that the minute the big guns stopped firing, an attack was coming. So, as soon as the guns fell silent, the Germans pushed their reserves forward, strengthening the line and making an advance almost impossible.

To prevent this, Brusilov attacked in several locations at once, preventing the enemy from knowing when the attack would come and where it would be strongest. Instead of a prolonged artillery barrage, the infantry and the artillery cooperated closely, picking the most essential targets to be destroyed as quickly as possible.

Brusilov's methods achieved a breakthrough. But because he wanted to preserve the element of surprise, the general could not concentrate large numbers of troops at any one point. And since supply lines could not keep up with the advancing infantry, the enemy could fall back and dig in elsewhere. So while Brusilov's tactics could poke a hole in the Central Powers' line, they could not destroy it.

German artillery advancing on Riga. The Germans used breakthrough methods to great effect on the Eastern Front, enabling them to smash holes in the Russian defense.

The end of the offensives marked a turning point in the war. The Austrians' poor performance convinced the Germans to take direct control. By September the Germans had taken supreme command of the Central Powers' armies. On the other side the Russian troops were weary, angry at their losses, and worried about their families. Rumors spread in the trenches that Russian civilians were starving. The discontent would have its repercussions in 1917. Only then would it become clear that Brusilov's advance had been the Imperial Army's last victory.

Women & Warfare

In the quest to keep up with the human and economic demands of modern warfare, the governments of Eastern Europe turned to women. Women become factory workers, administrators, and organizers – formerly male-dominated positions – showing political leaders that they were just as capable of contributing to the war effort as men.

By 1917 women made up around half of the labor force in Russia, and their share of the work in war-related industries, such as metal plants and mining, was still growing. Outside of the factory women staffed telegraph stations, operated streetcars, and took up the majority of office work. In some cases towns were populated almost entirely with working women.

Nursing was another activity in which Russian women of all classes participated, some, while serving at the front, at the cost of their lives. There were also a number of women fighting in combat, for example, the "Battalion of Death," and even a few pilots.

On the home front women excelled in support activities, working in the Red Cross or in various civic organizations. Such patriotic efforts took the form of caring for war widows and orphans, assisting the thousands of refugees who wandered the vast, bleak expanses of the country, and aiding Russian prisoners of war.

Women in Poland

In Poland women's activities were slightly different. They were less likely to be heavily involved in war industry: Since Polish manufacturing centers were very close to the front, they could not be relied upon by either side for

Russian refugees on a cart together with their worldly belongings in 1916.

supplies of war material. Polish women were, however, mobilized for factory work in the Polish territory controlled by Germany and Austria. In these regions women filled all sorts of positions left vacant by the thousands of men going off to fight.

Polish women played more important roles in the struggle for national independence. Women worked in several capacities in association with Polish political and civic groups after 1914. It was often women who took the initiative to organize or to staff support and medical services for Polish military forces.

During the war Polish women worked as clerks, couriers, instructors, journalists, mail carriers, medics, and supply procurers. They also worked as spies. Józef Piłsudski, the political activist seeking Poland's liberation from Russian control, employed women as intelligence operatives and couriers in his activities for Polish independence. Women proved to be highly successful in such endeavors, partly because neither the German nor the Russian military police would conduct strict personal searches of "young ladies."

Their brave activities helped Polish women win the right to vote in the independent Polish state after 1918, just as it did in the countries of Western Europe. Russian women enjoyed a period of even greater liberation after the war, a consequence of the Bolshevik Revolution of October 1917.

The Russian women's formidable "Battalion of Death" training in Petrograd around September 1917. The battalion was formed by the Provisional Government. The women fought in the Kerensky Offensive in July 1917, but left the Winter Palace to surrender to the Bolsheviks on the night of October 7–8, 1917. The rifle they carry is the shorter cavalry version of the Nagant, the standard Russian service rifle.

The TWO EMPERORS' MANIFESTO

A German attempt to win more recruits for its armies failed in its aim but gave the Poles new hope for independence.

The German and Austrian governors of Poland drive through Warsaw on their way to the Polish Regency Council.

The disastrous Brusilov Offensive left the Germans' opinion of the fighting skills of their Austrian allies – which had never been high – at a new low. Yet they still respected one part of the Austrian army: the Polish units. Since their formation in 1914, the Polish Legions, which numbered between 15,000 and 20,000 troops, had consistently distinguished themselves in battle. Even the demanding German commander Ludendorff recognized the Poles' fighting skill. For the Germans the question was how to make the best use of it.

In the spring of 1916 the Germans took a census which found that there were almost 1.5 million men living in the Polish lands in occupied Russia who were old enough to serve in the army. To the German military, who had suffered a severe shortage of manpower during the campaigns of 1916, Poland seemed a promising source of new recruits.

But how could the Germans persuade the Poles to fight for them? The German occupation of Poland after the Russian Great Retreat of 1915 had not been easy on the inhabitants. To satisfy their own war needs the Germans had nearly destroyed the Polish textile industry, as well as clearing many valuable forests for timber. Most Poles wanted nothing to do with the greedy occupier.

Planning Poland's future

Since the middle of 1915 the Germans and the Austrians had been negotiating Poland's future between them. The German Kaiser Wilhelm envisioned the re-creation of a Polish state linked to his own capital, Berlin. In August 1916 the two allies finally reached an agreement. After the war Poland would emerge as a constitutional kingdom, though it would be linked to the Central Powers both economically and militarily. On November 5, 1916, the German and Austrian emperors, Kaiser Wilhelm II and Franz Josef, issued a manifesto announcing their plan to the world.

A disappointing result

The German high command assumed that promising the Poles their independence would inevitably lead to a flood of Polish volunteers for military service in the German army. After all, the independence promised in the manifesto could only come with a victory for the Central Powers. But because they issued a call to sign up right after the publication of the "Two Em-

THE COMMANDERS

Józef Piłsudski 1867–1935
Polish politician
Socialist, political activist, and soldier, Piłsudski was considered by many to be the symbol of the struggle for Polish independence. Often regarded as the founder of the Polish state and armed forces, Piłsudski's major goal was always Polish freedom. A leading figure in the Polish Socialist Party in the 1890s, he later left the party in order to achieve his aims.

Based in Austrian Galicia before the war, Piłsudski organized an armed force to help gain Poland's independence. He served in the Austrian army during the war but felt no loyalty to the Austrians. Because of his disputes with Germany, he was arrested in July 1917 and spent the rest of the war in a German military prison.

After the war he became Poland's first head of state. In 1926 Piłsudski initiated authoritarian rule. He ran Poland until his death.

German troops mix with Polish villagers.

Crisis in Austria

At the start of the war the Austro-Hungarian government, like other governments, expected the conflict to be over in months. It saw no reason to stockpile the goods that it usually imported. But this left the empire vulnerable: It did not have enough supplies to survive a long war. Although Austria-Hungary had seen significant economic growth in the years before 1914, its population had increased at the same time. The empire could barely feed its own people. Austrians felt the effects of the British naval blockade almost as soon as war began. The textile industry, for example, which depended on foreign cotton and wool, was crippled.

The situation grew worse. Much of Austria's grain came from the eastern province of Galicia. But the grain fields were now a battleground. The size of the harvest halved in only three years. In early 1915 several Austrian cities, including the capital, Vienna, began to ration bread. The following year the government ordered citizens to go without meat for three days a week. By 1917 milk, sugar, coffee, and potatoes could only be obtained with ration cards. Officials noted that city dwellers "were eating half as much food as before the war." The shortages caused riots.

Hungry citizens of the Austrian capital, Vienna, stand in line for food at a soup kitchen.

Not only were the Austrians starving; they were freezing too. No coal was available because there were no railroad trains to bring it to the cities. During the severe winter of 1916 Austrians were only allowed to heat one room of their homes.

By the summer of 1917 the situation was critical. Shortages were getting worse and prices were rising. An official warned the emperor that the state could only survive the coming winter by increasing workers' rations. In fact, the government had to reduce them even more. At the turn of 1918 Austria appeared to be on the brink of collapse.

EYEWITNESS

As the crisis in Austria continued, an officer of the American embassy in Vienna noted the desperate conditions in a workers' district in March 1916:

66 I noticed strings of poorly dressed women and children held in line by police ... waiting for milk, vessel in hand.... Latecomers went home empty-handed, while lucky ones obtained only half as much as they expected. Similar lines ... can be observed standing in the morning ... in front of the bakers' shops and stores where coffee, tea, and sugar are being sold ... under the guarding eye of a police officer.... The worst feature ... is the scarcity in potatoes ... only such potatoes are available ... as are sold ... in the public markets ... half of them look as though not fit for consumption. 99

perors' Manifesto," the Poles felt that the Central Powers were simply manipulating them. Although the Germans had, indeed, created a provisional governing body for Poland, real political power still lay with the German military governor.

The attempt to milk Poland for recruits ended in failure. The German high command had expected to gain around 200,000 men; instead, just 14,000 volunteers signed up. More damaging still, the manifesto out-raged Russian conservatives who wanted to keep Poland as part of their empire. Their fury caused the breakdown of negotiations between Russia and Germany for a separate peace in the east.

For the Poles, however, the Germans' misjudgment promised much. The publication of the manifesto removed Poland's future from the Russians and thrust it into the international arena. There, a favorable decision seemed much more likely.

Polish refugees carry bundles of their possessions as they flee from villages caught up in the fighting.

WHERE TO FIND...

The FEBRUARY REVOLUTION

The problems of ordinary people in Russia exploded into strikes and protests. Radical politicians were ready to turn this uprising into a revolution.

Citizens and soldiers join in an antiwar demonstration in Petrograd in February 1917, shortly before the revolution began in earnest.

The sequence of changes that would transform Russia from a monarchy into the world's first communist state began in March 1917. Because Russia then used a different calendar, however, it is usually known as the February Revolution. Food shortages and strikes brought protesters onto the streets of the Russian capital, Petrograd, today called St. Petersburg. Within a few days the czar was forced to abdicate. He and his family were arrested. The 304-year rule of the Romanov dynasty in Russia came to an end.

Only two months earlier, at the start of 1917, the Russian high command had thought that prospects of victory were

80

EYEWITNESS

A Russian exile remembers what he saw of the protests that marked the beginning of the February Revolution:

66 If future historians look for the group that began the Russian Revolution, let them not create any involved theory. The Russian Revolution was begun by hungry women and children demanding bread and herrings. They started by wrecking tram cars and looting a few small shops. Only later did they, together with workmen and politicians, become ambitious to wreck that mighty edifice the Russian autocracy. 99

good. Russia's industries were producing large amounts of war materials. The tactics successfully used by General Brusilov in 1916 seemed to offer better chances of military victory; they were being adopted by commanders for the coming campaigns. In the overall war it was becoming clear that Russia and its allies were getting stronger than the Germans. More troops and more guns were available on every front. It seemed possible that an Allied victory might finally come by the end of the year.

The spirit of confidence, however, was undermined by crisis on the home front. Here things were falling apart. In the winter of 1916 a food shortage struck Petro-

A crowd of protesters scatters after coming under machine-gun fire at the beginning of the revolution in Petrograd. The army garrison in Petrograd, however, soon refused to fire on the protesters.

Far right: Lenin addresses a crowd in Moscow's Red Square in 1919, when he was leader of the new Soviet Union.

The Bolsheviks

The Bolsheviks, a Russian word that means "those in the majority," first emerged on the Russian political scene in 1903 as a group within the Social Democratic Party. The Bolsheviks, led by Lenin, believed that a revolution was necessary to create the just and equal society that they wanted to bring into existence. They argued that the party should be composed of dedicated revolutionaries. Lenin had explained his views in a pamphlet written in 1902, *What Is To Be Done*. He called on revolutionaries to take the lead in creating a mass movement to overthrow the czarist government. This position split the Social Democratic Party. The opposing group were the Mensheviks, or "those in the minority." They preferred a more gradual strategy. But it was the radical Bolsheviks who would take power in Russia in November 1917.

Bolshevik deputies pose in their prison uniforms after being arrested in 1914 by the czar's secret police for opposing the war. The men, who were exiled to Siberia, had served in the first Duma in 1905 and in subsequent assemblies.

grad. Rocketing prices made the shortage worse. Industrial workers worried that their wages could not keep up with the cost of living.

The thoughts of the workers of Petrograd were important. More than 400,000 people toiled in war-related industries in or near the capital. They accounted for almost 25 percent of Russia's industrial output. They demanded improved working conditions. They also wanted political changes, insisting on the creation of a government capable of running the war effort efficiently. Angry workers had staged more than 1,100 strikes between the summer of 1915 and February 1917.

Other fears and suspicions also fueled tensions. Rumors spread through Petrograd: The czar's "German" wife was leading the state to ruin while he was away

WAR PROFILES

Vladimir Ilyich Lenin
1870–1924
Russian politician

Lenin was the founder of the Bolshevik party and the guiding force of the Russian Revolution.

Lenin, whose real name was V.I. Ulyanov, became a revolutionary when he was a young man. He was forced to live in exile from 1905 to 1917. After the February Revolution he returned to Russia to help lead the Bolshevik seizure of power.

Lenin became the head of the new communist government after the October revolution in 1917. He fought off counterrevolutionaries in a civil war that lasted from 1918 to 1920. Lenin ruled the new Soviet Union until his death. For better or worse, Lenin was one of the architects of the 20th-century world.

commanding the armies; the rich could get all the food they wanted. Such stories helped drive the citizens of Petrograd into the streets in protest.

The events that resulted in the overthrow of the czarist government began on March 8, according to the modern Gregorian calendar used in most of the world. Russia was then still using the old Julian calendar, according to which the date was February 23, which gave the revolution its Russian name.

March 8 was International Women's Day. In Petrograd women marched to demand bread. They were joined by strikers, who also got their comrades to stop work. The protests grew. On March 10 more than 200,000 people marched during a strike that paralyzed the city.

The authorities tried to stop the protests. But the soldiers of the Petrograd garrison refused to act against the protesters. It was a crucial turning point. Some Cossack units even defended the crowd against the czar's dreaded police. By March 12 the city was in the hands of the revolutionaries.

In response to the crisis Czar Nicholas ordered the Duma, or parliament, to dissolve itself. Instead parliamentary deputies decided to form a provisional government. Some genuinely welcomed the opportunity to govern the country; others only wanted to bring the disturbances under control. One conservative deputy made clear his determination to stop radicals gaining influence: "If we don't take power others will take it, those who have already elected some scoundrels in the factories."

Meantime army commanders advised the czar to give up the throne for Russia's sake. On March 15 Nicholas abdicated in favor of his brother, Michael. The following day Michael stepped down, turning power over to the Duma. Within a week Nicholas and his family were arrested. The Romanov family's rule in Russia was over.

The former czar is guarded by soldiers during his exile.

Provisional Government in RUSSIA

The Provisional Government tried to bring order to Russia and continue the war. Its failure brought revolution.

Russia's Provisional Government was formed on March 15, 1917, to replace the monarchy. It was headed by Prince Georgii Lvov and made up of members of the National Assembly, or Duma, and other leaders. The government included people of all political views, except the revolutionary Bolsheviks and monarchist supporters of the czar.

Its aim was to run the country until a constituent assembly could be elected. Unlike the previous Duma this would be a democratically elected body representing all of Russia's social and ethnic groups. The constituent assembly would decide the future form of Russia's government.

During its brief existence the Provisional Government granted Russia's citizens freedom of assembly, of speech, and of religion. It issued orders to free all political prisoners and, after discussion, it abolished the death penalty. This was controversial because some members wanted to execute some of the royal family. The Provisional Government also attempted to reorganize local and regional government, and tried to ensure equal rights for the country's non-Russian minorities.

The government's political problems, however, were insurmountable. From the

politics

The Duma

The National Assembly, or Duma, was created by Czar Nicholas II after the failure of the revolution in Russia in 1905. But it turned out to be ineffective and failed to represent the Russian people. The czar gave it authority to pass laws and regulate part of the national budget, but he kept the right to veto any laws passed by the assembly. Military expenditure, nearly 40 percent of the budget, was still controlled by Nicholas and his ministers. Government officials were responsible to the czar alone, not to the Duma.

In March 1917 the limited authority given to the Duma turned out to have major consequences. Members of the Duma did not feel it was their place to decide on vital issues such as land reform. They believed that the new constituent assembly should give the state its direction. The Duma missed its chance to make radical changes. It would be left to a small group of determined revolutionaries, the Bolsheviks, to do so.

very beginning it had to deal with a powerful rival: the Petrograd Soviet of Workers' and Soldiers' Deputies. The Soviet – the Russian word means council – did not oppose the government outright but it often acted independently in ways that contradicted government plans.

It especially undermined the authority of the army high command by issuing Order Number One. This declared that military units ought to be run by elected committees, not by officers. Soon Soviets cropped up all over Russia. The councils were better able to relate to the people than the far-off government in Petrograd.

The Provisional Government weathered crisis after crisis, however, until it fell on November 7, 1917. Then another revolution would change the future of Russia.

Prince Lvov, who was named prime minister of the new Provisional Government in 1917.

WHERE TO FIND...

**February
    Revolution: 6:**80
Bolsheviks: 6:82
**Kerensky
    Offensive: 6:**94
**October
    Revolution:
    6:**100

The Czech Independence Campaign

Developments in the war confirmed the weakness of Austria-Hungary. This benefited the Czech leaders who were campaigning for their people's independence.

Far right: During World War I Edvard Beneš worked for Czech independence as general secretary of the Czechoslovak National Council.

The prospects for the creation of an independent Czechoslovak state appeared much brighter by mid-1917. Czech leaders Tomáš Masaryk and Edvard Beneš were campaigning in Britain and France to gain support for Czech independence. After initial indifference they were beginning to get real results.

Tomáš Masaryk had represented Czech nationalist political parties in the Austrian parliament before World War I. After the war he became the first president of Czechoslovakia.

Masaryk, for example, met leading French politicians in 1916. He impressed them with his ideas for the postwar reconstruction of Europe. These ideas included the formation of an independent state for the Czechs and Slovaks. Appointed as a professor at the University of London in October 1916, Masaryk wrote several influential articles in *The New Europe*, a journal devoted to transforming Austria-Hungary into a group of independent states. But the British government hesitated to support the idea of breaking up Austria-Hungary.

Meanwhile, other factors began to change British and French attitudes. German schemes to dominate eastern and central Europe, which the Germans called *Mitteleuropa*, encouraged the Allies to take Czech plans more seriously.

The Czech cause also received a boost in November 1916 with the

The Western powers also realized that Austria was becoming increasingly dominated by Germany. This potential growth in German influence seemed to give them no choice but to support a break up of Austria-Hungary. By 1918 Beneš had got them to declare that the "Czecho-Slovak" peoples should be "liberated from foreign domination."

Throughout their stay in the west Masaryk and Beneš acted as though they represented both the Czech and the Slovak peoples. Yet even by 1918 they could not show that this was really so. An agreement between Czech and Slovak immigrant groups living in the United States changed the situation.

The Pittsburgh Convention of May 1918 made several promises to the Slovaks in return for their support of a future Czechoslovak state. They would have their own civil administration and court system; Slovak would be the official language of the Slovakian part of the country.

This agreement would be a source of controversy after the war, when the Czechs and the Slovaks argued over its legal value. For the moment, however, it gave Masaryk what he needed: the appearance, at least, that both the Czechs and the Slovaks wanted to break away from Austria and form their own separate state.

reelection of Woodrow Wilson as president of the United States. Like the British, Wilson hesitated to break up Austria-Hungary, but his views about the right of peoples to choose their own form of government inspired the Czechs to press on with their claims.

Masaryk and Beneš were campaigning in exile, but calls for independence also came from Czech nationalists who had remained behind. The success of the February Revolution in Russia in 1917 encouraged Czech politicians in Austria to demand that the Austro-Hungarian empire be converted into "a federation of free and equal states."

Austrian PEACE INITIATIVES

Austria-Hungary's new emperor tried to take his country out of the war but was compelled to fight on, relying even more heavily on his German allies.

Far right: Emperor Karl of Austria had served as an army officer on the Eastern Front and in Italy before he came to the throne.

The death of the Emperor Franz Josef on November 21, 1916, brought his grandnephew Karl to the Austro-Hungarian throne. Like his great-uncle, the new emperor understood that, in the course of the war, Austria had become excessively dependent on its powerful German ally. And, again like Franz Josef, Karl thoroughly resented the patronizing attitude the Germans took toward the Austrians. In response he tried to assert his country's independence.

Independent policies

Earlier in the war the Austrians had been forced to put their army under a joint command with the Germans. This effectively put the Germans in charge. Immediately after he came to the throne Karl took the Austrian army out of this command. He also spoke out against Germany's decision to resume unrestricted submarine warfare in the Atlantic.

By early 1917 the war had lost its meaning for the Hapsburg monarchy. The original hope that the conflict would unite the empire's ethnic minorities had long since faded. Karl now had to devote all his energies to keeping the empire in one piece. The new emperor's boldest step was to approach Britain, France, and Italy with a proposal for peace. The United States was not included because the U.S. did not actually declare war on Austria until the end of the year.

Using his brother-in-law, Prince Sixtus of Parma, as an intermediary Karl tried to open peace negotiations with the French without the Germans knowing. Sixtus was then serving in the Belgian army but he had French citizenship and access to political leaders in France. Karl first made contact with the Allies in February 1917.

According to the proposals that Sixtus passed on, Austria sought no territorial gains from the war. Serbia, which it had occupied, would be restored. Karl insisted only on guarantees for Austria's security. In return Karl promised that he would mediate with the Germans regarding French claims to their former provinces of Alsace and Lorraine.

Dissent within the empire

Making quick progress toward peace was urgent for Karl. After the February Revolution in Russia demands for constitutional change from the Czechs, Croats, and other subject peoples in the Austrian empire got louder and more insistent.

WAR PROFILES

Karl I
1887–1922
Austro-Hungarian
emperor

Karl would have lived his whole life as an army officer but for the assassination of his uncle, Archduke Franz Ferdinand, in 1914. As heir to the throne he continued to serve in the army until the death of Franz Josef in 1916.

After he became emperor Karl made repeated unsuccessful efforts to get Austria out of the war. His last bid to save the empire was a proclamation in October 1918 which reorganized Austria-Hungary into a federal state. The peoples of the empire chose instead to break away and form independent countries.

Karl refused to abdicate formally and fled to Switzerland in March 1919. He twice tried to return to Hungary as king but failed. He died in 1922.

But although the French and the British seemed willing to consider the Austrian proposals the Italians would not agree. They demanded several towns and regions from Austria, including the important port of Trieste. Karl might have been willing to give up some territory to Italy, but he wanted to hold on to Trieste. The secret negotiations finally broke down on this point in early June.

In the spring of the next year, 1918, the French made part of the Prince Sixtus negotiations public. This forced Karl to deny everything, and to pledge his commitment to the Austro-German alliance. The only result of Austrian efforts to follow an independent policy turned out to be an even greater reliance on Germany. The Austrians had little option but to continue the fight and hope for a German victory.

POLAND

WAR PROFILES

Ignacy Jan Paderewski 1860–1941

Polish politician

Ever since the spring of 1915, when international pianist Ignacy Jan Paderewski made his latest visit to the United States, he had devoted his energies to explaining and promoting the Polish cause. He spoke passionately and enthusiastically not only to Polish immigrant groups but also to American political leaders. He conferred with President Wilson's special advisor, Colonel House, on several occasions, and also met with the president himself. By 1917 he had become the recognized spokesperson of the Polish nation in America.

In independent Poland Paderewski was the prime minister of the government in 1919. In 1921 he decided to return to his life as an artist. He became active in politics once again only in the late 1930s, when he joined a group that opposed the Piłsudski-dominated government.

A Polish woman stands in her ruined village, destroyed in the war.

Toward Polish
INDEPENDENCE

The collapse of the czarist regime in Russia gave new impetus to the Polish move for independence. Yet the real power in Poland remained with Germany and Austria.

The February Revolution in Russia in 1917 prompted Czech politicians to call for greater rights in Austria. The events in Russia, however, did even more for the Polish cause. Within days after the collapse of the czarist regime, the Russian Provisional Government issued a manifesto recognizing the right of the Poles to become an independent state. Yet the Provisional Government assumed that its

Western allies would keep Russian interests in mind, which meant preserving some degree of Russian influence in Poland. Such concerns dictated how the French dealt with Polish politicians like Roman Dmowski, who were operating in France.

In June 1917 the Poles were allowed to create their own army on French soil, but this gesture was meant to keep Polish activities under French – and Russian – control. In August, however, Dmowski created the Polish National Committee. The next month the French recognized the committee as the official Polish representative to the Western powers and the other Allies later did the same. In the meantime

Józef Piłsudski, leader of the movement for Polish independence. He commanded Poland's armed forces when the Central Powers established Poland as a semi-autonomous state in November 1916. After being arrested by the Germans in 1917, he spent the rest of the war in a German military prison.

Ignacy Jan Paderewski, a concert pianist and patron of the Polish arts, had been touring the United States, seeking to publicize and gain support for the Polish cause.

Operating on Polish territory, Józef Piłsudski recognized the February Revolution as the collapse of Russian power. He saw the Central Powers as the main obstacle to Polish independence. In the spring of 1917 Piłsudski worked to undermine German plans. The crisis came in July when he and his supporters refused to take an oath pledging "brotherhood in arms" with Germany and Austria. The Germans broke up the Polish Legions and arrested Piłsudski.

In October the Central Powers created a Regency Council. The council, made up of three conservative Poles, was supposed to function as the main branch of the Polish state. In reality its control was limited. The Central Powers could veto its legislation. Real political power in Poland was in the hands of the Germans and Austrians, and would remain there until the fall of 1918.

WHERE TO FIND...

February Revolution: 6:80

Piłsudski: 6:77

Dmowski: 6:45

Polish Activism: 6:44

Two Emperors' Manifesto: 6:76

Collapse of Austria-Hungary: 6:114

ANTIWAR PROTEST in Russia

In the summer of 1917 the new government in Russia faced a worsening economic situation and growing popular unrest.

After the Russian Provisional Government took power in March 1917, it began to pass liberal legislation. By doing so it unleashed a revolutionary fervor in Russia.

Throughout the country people formed political groups that pressed for democratic or socialist reforms. Public meetings, rallies, and speeches all drew enthusiastic crowds. There was much to demonstrate about. Russia's economy was collapsing and the new leaders were having little success in improving the situation. Most of their policies had only added to the people's hardship.

Inflation was one of the greatest problems. Prices were out of control and many goods could only be bought on the black market for extortionate amounts. After just six months of the new government's

Bolshevik workers and soldiers on a political march in Petrograd on June 18, 1917. The socialist Bolsheviks were behind many of the antigovernment demonstrations during the war.

Russians make deals on the black market – a place where illicit goods are bought and sold – in a Moscow courtyard. The black market was often the only place to buy certain items, although they could be very expensive.

rule, the Russian currency, the ruble, was worth only half of its previous value.

People in the cities were also hungry. The harvest of 1917 had been poor and there were severe food shortages. By fall bread rations in Petrograd had to be cut from one pound per day to a half pound.

Transport difficulties made the situation worse. The rail network had almost ground to a standstill and it was very difficult to ship merchandise between cities. Factories gave any goods that they could not move to locals in exchange for food.

Things were worse in the countryside. Russia's peasants were in revolt. When the government hesitated with land reforms, the peasants took matters into their own hands. Many seized landowners' property and shared it among themselves. Some peasants also attacked government officials who tried to collect grain as a tax to support the war effort.

The Russians were tired of the war. The socialist Bolsheviks led demands for an end to the fighting. In June 1917 an army officer observed: "If you were to go out on the village square and proclaim that the war will end at once, but only on condition that the czar returns to power, every single man would agree and there would be no more talk of a democratic republic."

In July 1917 the antiwar feeling erupted into mass protest when the government again called on Russian men to take up arms. They were needed for an offensive that the minister of war, Aleksandr Kerensky, hoped would push the Central Powers out of Russia once and for all.

WHERE TO FIND...

Provisional Government: 6:84

Bolsheviks: 6:82

Kerensky: 6:95

February Revolution: 6:80

Prewar Russia: 1:42

The KERENSKY OFFENSIVE

In summer 1917 the Russian government planned a military campaign that would defeat the enemy and unite the country.

Far right: Aleksandr Kerensky, who became Russian minister of war in June 1917. Here he is shown sitting in his cabinet office in Petrograd, the Russian capital.

When the Russian Provisional Government came to power, the Allies were quick to recognize the new regime. With a constitutional republic in Russia it was easier for Britain

A map shows the Russians' original plans for the Kerensky Offensive in the southern and the northern sectors of the front. A lack of troops, however, restricted the attack to Galicia in the south.

Map

0 — 100 miles

Riga

East Prussia

Vilna

Brest–Litovsk

RUSSIA

Lemberg

Galicia

AUSTRIA-HUNGARY

and France to portray the war as a fight between democracy and repression. The new Russian leaders, for their part, promised to continue the war.

Promising to continue fighting was one thing; keeping the promise was another. The new government was facing a collapsing economy and there was unrest throughout the country. The Russian people were tired of the war. Bolshevik-led rallies called for an end to the conflict. In March 1917 the Petrograd Soviet – a radical council which was the government's main political rival – issued a statement calling for peace.

Discontent at home was matched within the armed forces at the front. Since the Provisional Government had taken power, the morale of the troops had fallen. The desertion rate had increased fivefold. There had been little activity on the Eastern Front for months and the soldiers were bored and hungry. Bolshevik and German propaganda convinced them that the Germans would not attack and they could see no sense in continuing the war. Discipline declined. The troops formed soldiers' committees, which permitted them to elect their own officers and to vote on command decisions.

planned a renewed campaign against the Central Powers. He thought that it would not only improve the morale of the army but would also unite the country. In June 1917 he appointed General Alexei Brusilov as commander in chief of the Russian armies and together they planned a major offensive.

Their plan was to repeat the Brusilov Offensive of 1916. The Russians would attack first in Galicia in the southern sector of the front. They would then strike further north near Vilna and push the Germans out of Russia for good.

Almost at once the plan faced strong opposition. Many soldiers refused to take part. Some agreed to fight on one condition: That they could execute their officers if the offensive failed. On July 1, 1917, a

The government needed to act to prevent the further disintegration of the army. The minister of war, Aleksandr Kerensky,

behind the lines

Trench propaganda

Before the Kerensky Offensive, Bolshevik supporters at the front distributed antiwar leaflets among the trenches urging the soldiers to stop the fighting. This is an example:

"Brothers! We beg you not to obey an order that is meant to destroy us. An offensive is planned. Take no part in it. Our old leaders have no authority now. Our officers want to make an end of us. They are the traitors. They are the internal enemy. They would like everything to be as before. You know well that all our generals have been put on reduced pay and they want this revenge.

"We shall be thrown back when we reach the enemy's wire. We cannot break through. I have reconnoitered in the enemy lines and I know well that there are ten rows of it with machine guns every 15 yards. It is useless to advance. If we do, we shall be dead men with nobody left to hold our front. Pass this on, brothers, and … write other letters of the same sort."

women

Battalion of Death

Before the Provisional Government took power, women played a limited role in the Russian armed forces. Normally they only served as military drivers. They rarely fought at the front.

But the revolutionary atmosphere of 1917 allowed women to make a much greater contribution. In May of that year the Russian authorities gave Mariya Bochkareva permission to form all-women units. Bochkareva had already fought at the front and had earned herself a reputation for bravery.

Within days Bochkareva had organized two 1,000-strong units in Petrograd. She named the units the "Women's Battalion of Death," stressing the women's willingness to die in defense of Russia.

But Bochkareva's strict discipline prompted many of her recruits to have second thoughts. Bolshevik agitation also undermined her efforts. Soon only 300 women soldiers remained.

Bochkareva's women fought in the Kerensky Offensive in July 1917. They captured 2,000 Austrian prisoners before hostility from male soldiers forced them to disband. But the idea of women's units spread. By fall 1917 around 5,000 women were serving in the Russian army.

A Russian woman soldier goes through her drill. Many women showed extreme bravery in the face of the enemy but their success often provoked opposition from their male colleagues.

massive demonstration in Petrograd demanded peace.

That same day the Kerensky Offensive began. Having recruited fewer troops than they had planned, the Russians were restricted to two main thrusts in Galicia. Brusilov's two armies – the Seventh and Eleventh – attacked along a 50-mile front. Five days later General Lavrenti Kornilov

age of supplies, a lack of reinforcements, and extreme exhaustion had slowed the Russian advance to a crawl.

On July 19 the Germans counterattacked. They met little resistance. Apart from a few elite units, the Russian soldiers had lost their stomach for battle. Tens of thousands of them simply threw down their weapons and walked away. The

A Russian soldier drives two deserters back toward the front line with the butt of his rifle.

led the Eighth Army in an attack further south along the Dniester River in the foothills of the Carpathian Mountains.

Initially the Russians were very successful. They pushed the Central Powers back nearly 30 miles toward Lemberg in Austria-Hungary. On the first day of the offensive alone the Russians took around 10,000 prisoners. But by mid-July a short-

Germans drove the remaining Russians back to beyond their original positions.

The Kerensky Offensive was a complete failure. Instead of improving the soldiers' morale, it hastened the collapse of the army. It increased the people's hostility to the government and widened the country's deep social divisions. It was Russia's last major action of the war.

The Kerensky Offensive **97**

The Fall of
RIGA

In September 1917 the Germans captured Russia's second largest port on the Baltic Sea. It would be the final time the two armies would meet in the war.

The German response to the Kerensky Offensive was not limited to the southern sector of the front. The Germans decided to attack in the north, too. Riga, a Baltic port, was their target.

Both sides recognized Riga's strategic importance. Although the port was 300 miles from Petrograd, the Russian capital, little stood between the two cities. If the Germans could capture Riga and trap the

defending Russian Twelfth Army, they could advance on Petrograd. The Russians would then have to ask for peace.

Toward the end of August 1917 the Germans moved large numbers of troops from the Galician front in the south to positions around Riga. There they joined General Oskar von Hutier's Eighth Army, which was already in the area preparing for the offensive.

New tactics

The operation would give the Germans an opportunity to test a new method of attack. They had been trying to work out how to mount an assault in the face of tremendous enemy firepower. In the end they came up with a plan similar to the one that the Russians had used in the Brusilov Offensive of 1916.

Like the Russians, the Germans would use the cover of heavy artillery to make a massive forward advance. But they would add something new: stormtrooper battalions. These were small units of specially trained men armed with light machine guns, grenades, and flamethrowers. The stormtroopers would infiltrate the enemy lines ahead of the main assault and destroy the weakest points. The method became known as the "Hutier tactics."

An easy victory

The Germans struck on September 1, 1917. They met with immediate success. On the first day they crossed the Dvina River, the major natural obstacle between them and Riga. The following day they had the entire city under their control. They met very lit-

tle resistance. The Russians had learned of the German attack and prepared their retreat. When the strike came, the defenders fled so quickly that the Germans captured only 9,000 prisoners.

Although von Hutier's troops pursued the fleeing Russians, they soon abandoned the chase. Circumstances had changed. They no longer needed to reach Petrograd

and demand the surrender of the Russian government. The Russians had ceased to pose a real military threat. Amid growing civil unrest, Russia was rapidly falling apart. The remnants of the Twelfth Army – virtually the only effective Russian force left – were transferred from the front line to Petrograd, where they were needed to quell the disorder in the city.

With the exception of a few minor operations, the fall of Riga marked the final military engagement on the Eastern Front between the German and Russian armies. Russia's involvement in World War I was almost over but her internal problems were only just beginning.

German soldiers pick through equipment left behind by the Russians in their withdrawal from Riga.

Far left: Germans build a bridge over the Dvina River on September 1, 1917.

WHERE TO FIND...
Brusilov Offensive: 6:62
Flamethrowers: 7:48
Antiwar Protest in Russia: 6:92

The OCTOBER REVOLUTION

As the Bolsheviks gathered public support, Lenin waited for the right moment to bring down the Provisional Government.

Over the course of 1917, while the Provisional Government was forced to deal with crisis after crisis, the Bolsheviks slowly gained support. They constantly protested against the war, insisted that factories be run by workers' councils, and demanded that all political power be given to the Soviets – elected governmental councils. The Bolsheviks also promised to confiscate the land of the great estates and divide it among the Russian peasantry.

By making these demands Lenin's party began to appeal to workers and soldiers;

Revolutionary workers and soldiers guard the the Smolny Institute which housed the headquarters of the Bolshevik Party, the headquarters of the revolution in Petrograd, during the October 1917 Revolution.

the majority of soldiers were peasants. Lenin's party was especially appealing since the Provisional Government insisted on continuing the war and delaying the redistribution of land. As it gathered support, the Bolshevik Party inched closer to its ultimate goal: The overthrow of the Provisional Government and the creation of the world's first communist state.

The return of Lenin

Lenin, exiled in Zurich, Switzerland, since the 1905 revolution, first arrived in Petrograd in mid-April 1917. The Germans had smuggled him into Russia by rail. Eager to disrupt the Russian war effort, the German government believed that Lenin's antiwar views would contribute to Russia's domestic turmoil. So, on the condition that he did not try to spread revolutionary ideas on German territory, the Germans whisked Lenin across Germany to Russia in a sealed train, together with his wife and 27 other Bolsheviks.

Power did not come easily to the Bolsheviks. Arriving in Russia via Finland, Lenin discovered that some members of the party were cooperating with the Provisional Government. These members believed that the Provisional Government had to be protected from a counterrevolution by forces loyal to the czar.

But Lenin would have none of this. In his first statement upon arriving, the stern "April Thesis," he argued that the capitalist system had already run its course in Russia, and that the time was ripe for the socialist revolution. He demanded that his fellow Bolsheviks withdraw their support for the Provisional Government and agitate for an immediate end to the war.

At first Lenin's arguments were received with a good deal of skepticism, even from members of his own party. His repu-

Red Army men use an armored cargo tramcar for transporting arms to the places where the fighting was taking place during the October Revolution in Moscow.

tation also suffered when it was made public that he had been helped in his journey to Russia by the hated Germans. He would struggle throughout his career to get rid of this connection. Nevertheless Lenin was eventually able to persuade his fellow Bolsheviks that his way was the right one. By the end of April the All-Russian Bolshevik Conference adopted Lenin's ideas as its official program.

Still, the road to power was a long one. Although they were gaining in support through their appeals to the masses, the Bolsheviks failed in their first attempt to seize control of Russia. This occurred during the "July days," from July 16 to 18. Armed soldiers and sailors, urged on by the Bolsheviks and joined by an undirected mob, marched into Petrograd in order to overthrow the Provisional Government. But the demonstration failed when the Petrograd Soviet refused to endorse it and some military units insisted on remaining loyal to the government.

The accusation that the German military had been giving instructions and funding to the Bolsheviks surfaced again, and a crackdown on the revolutionaries ensued.

alternatives

What if the German high command had not allowed Lenin to travel to Russia? The Russian Revolution may have taken an entirely different course had he not arrived in Petrograd in April 1917. It was Lenin who persuaded the Bolsheviks to alter their tactics and bid for power in October. The provisional government might not have survived in any event: It may have fallen to more radical elements sooner or later, since the political right was fragmented. Lenin might have returned to influence events at a later date. But by helping Lenin the Germans made the collapse of Kerensky's government a certainty.

Lenin fled to Finland, where he remained until October 23. His associate Trotsky, meanwhile, was arrested.

On July 21 Aleksandr Kerensky became prime minister. He would have little time to settle in. After Riga fell in September, effectively ending Russia's military efforts, Kerensky came into conflict with General Lavrenti Kornilov, the latest commander in chief of the Russian armed forces.

The "Kornilov affair"

Kornilov insisted on a number of measures designed to strengthen discipline in the disintegrating armed forces. Kerensky, already irritated that the general had the support of right-wing politicians, took Kornilov's demands as a sure sign of counterrevolution. The general, meanwhile, scorned Kerensky's inability to act decisively when Russia was in peril.

On September 8 Kornilov was dismissed. The general marched on Petrograd, rapidly reaching the outskirts. Kerensky announced that Kornilov had launched an attack on the government and appealed to the people of Petrograd "to save the revolution." Workers and soldiers prepared to defend the capital. Kornilov's forces melted away in the face of determined opposition. The general, persuaded to surrender on September 14, was arrested. He would later join the White forces fighting the Bolsheviks. Kerensky had crushed the attempted right-wing coup.

American journalist John Silas Reed.

WAR PROFILES ○

**Leon Trotsky
1879–1940
Russian politician**
Known for his effectiveness as a speaker and for his abilities to plan and organize, Trotsky – whose real name was Lev Bronstein – had been closely associated with the revolutionary movement in Russia since the early 1900s.

Lenin's political and military preparations for the October Revolution were of vital importance to the Bolshevik cause. After the Bolshevik rise to power Trotsky served as the first commissar of foreign affairs, negotiating the Treaty of Brest-Litovsk with the Germans.

Later Trotsky became commissar for war, building the hastily constructed Red Army into an effective fighting force. Losing a power struggle to Joseph Stalin in the late 1920s, Trotsky went into exile. He was assassinated by Stalin's agents in Mexico in 1940.

Above right: Leon Trotsky.

But Kerensky now lost any support that he had from the political right. On the left the Petrograd Soviet from this point on suspected the prime minister himself of having been in league with Kornilov against the revolution.

The Bolsheviks gain support

The winners of the "Kornilov affair" were the Bolsheviks. Kerensky, seeking increased support from the left, released Trotsky and other Bolshevik leaders from prison. The Red Guard, given weapons by the prime minister to protect the city against Kornilov, would come to take the side of the Bolsheviks when disorder broke out again. The masses, not trusting Kerensky, shifted their support to the Bolsheviks.

By mid-September the Bolsheviks had won majorities in both the Petrograd and Moscow Soviets. Lenin, still in Finland, wrote urgently to his comrades that the moment had come: Now was the time to seize power.

He met with stiff opposition. A number of Bolsheviks argued against a grab for power, contending that a revolt might be suppressed by counterrevolutionary forces. This group also claimed that the Bolsheviks did not have widespread support. They believed that it would be better to win power slowly, by legal means. In order to convince his colleagues, Lenin arrived in Petrograd, in disguise, on October 23. Although some Bolsheviks remained hesitant, Lenin managed to persuade the executive committee of the party that his view was the right one.

The moment arrives

Although the Bolsheviks had made a decision, they had yet to set a date to act. Kerensky provided the Bolsheviks with the pretext that they needed. On the

the armies

Red Army

The inability of Bolshevik forces to disarm the Czech troops left in Russia after the collapse of the Imperial Army made the Bolsheviks realize that they needed an army. Now that they had destroyed the Russian Imperial Army through agitation and propaganda, it became imperative to build up a military force that would be loyal to the cause of the October Revolution.

The task went to Trotsky, people's commissar for war. First Trotsky recruited officers from the old czarist army to serve in the Bolshevik Red Army. By the end of the year 22,295 former officers and 128,168 former NCOs had signed up. Trotsky also introduced conscription. As in the old imperial army, discipline was strictly enforced. Trotsky introduced a system of political commissars who countersigned every order that was issued.

The Red Army soon shaped into a formidable fighting force. It rapidly grew in size, due to conscription, from 400,000 in 1919 to over 5 million after 1920. The new army would defend the gains of October and help to spread them across Russia.

Members of the Workers' and Peasants' University undergo their training for the Red Army, 1918.

evening of November 5 – October 23 by the old Russian calendar, hence the name October Revolution – the Provisional Government decided to close two Bolshevik newspapers for instigating an uprising. Kerensky ordered the arrest of the Bolsheviks who had taken part in the attempted "July days" uprising and were plotting against the government. Lenin's party used this as an excuse to launch the fight against the counterrevolution.

Left: In Palace Square, Petrograd, the Bolsheviks address a meeting of many thousands of workers and soldiers. The Bolsheviks appealed to the ordinary Russian public by addressing issues relevant to their everyday life, such as the ownership of land, the redistribution of wealth, and the running of factories.

The Bolsheviks seize power

By the morning of November 7 troops, sailors, and Red Guards loyal to the Petrograd Soviet took over key points in the city. The occupiers encountered no opposition: Government forces proved to be ineffectual. Even though government ministers remained undisturbed at the Winter Palace, at 10:00 a.m. Lenin issued a proclamation which stated that all political power had been assumed by the Petrograd Soviet.

During the night of November 7–8 (October 25–26) the Second All-Russian Congress of Soviets approved the Bolshevik coup. Despite the protest of moderate socialists, who walked out of the congress – scornfully mocked by Trotsky – power was handed over to the Bolsheviks.

Lenin takes control

In the early hours of November 8 a small detachment of troops entered the Winter Palace and arrested the remaining ministers: Kerensky had already left the capital to seek loyal reinforcements. A few hours later a Bolshevik government was formed, and control of the Russian capital Petrograd passed into the hands of Vladimir Ilyich Lenin.

The WHITE REBELLION

As the Bolsheviks tightened their hold on Russia, counter-revolutionary forces – the Whites – rose up against them.

Counterrevolutionaries from Georgia, in the Caucasus Mountains, prepare to defend their new state. The Bolsheviks took control of Georgia in 1921.

I n the first weeks of November 1917 the Bolsheviks seized power in the Russian capital, Petrograd. Yet outside the city things were different. Across Russia Lenin's party had taken control in some areas but was ineffective in others.

Bolshevik strength was greatest in the cities in the central part of the country. At first there was little opposition to the takeover. Yet in the regions far away from the capital there were many opponents to Bolshevik rule. The radical plans of the

Bolsheviks, together with their fierce repression of rival parties, soon fired strong opposition. Many would also turn against the revolutionaries when they signed the Treaty of Brest-Litovsk in March 1918, surrendering to Germany.

These various forces of counterrevolution, known collectively as the Whites, were united only in their determination to rid Russia of the Bolsheviks, or Reds. The White armies were also supported and supplied by Britain and France, who, driven by their distrust and fear of socialism, wanted to end Bolshevik rule.

The Whites' revolt

The first armed revolt against Lenin's government broke out on the Don River in December 1917. This was the uprising of the Don Cossacks, led by General Lavrenti Georgievich Kornilov and General Aleksei Kaledin. Kornilov had commanded the Russian forces under the Provisional Government in July but then turned against Kerensky and joined the Don Cossacks, an anti-Bolshevik army. After the death of both these officers – Kornilov was struck by an artillery shell during the fighting and Kaledin committed suicide after a defeat – General Anton Denikin took up the fight in the south.

Elsewhere anti-Bolshevik forces forged an alliance with the Czechoslovak Legion, which took control of the vital communications route, the Trans-Siberian railroad, in mid-1918.

The activities of the White forces in late 1917 and early 1918 were only the beginning of a cruel and exhausting civil war that would seize Russia through 1920. The White movement was a grave threat to the Bolshevik government. In October 1919 counterrevolutionary forces threatened Petrograd and Moscow – which had become the capital in March 1918 – simultaneously. Yet the Whites were incapable of dealing Lenin's regime a death blow.

The people fight back

The Red Army was stronger in military terms, but this only partly explains the defeat of the Whites. Equally important was the insistence of counterrevolutionary commanders on restoring the old order. For the non-Russians promised self-determination by the Bolsheviks this meant a return to Russian rule. And for peasants guaranteed their own land by the Bolsheviks it meant returning this newly acquired property to the landlords.

The majority of Russians opted for the future, not a return to the past. As a result Russia would remain communist – an extreme form of socialism, which the Bolsheviks adopted as their policy – for the next 70 years.

Left: Officer cadets in the Kremlin, Moscow, in November 1917, prepare to stop revolutionary workers.

ARMISTICE

As soon as he had gained power, Lenin sought peace with Germany. Although the Russian people welcomed the end of the fighting, the price of this peace would be high.

Freezing and desperate Russian troops buy secondhand goods during an armistice on December 15, 1917.

As he had promised, Lenin issued a decree of peace as one of the first acts of the new Bolshevik government. His decree came immediately after the fall of the Provisional Government.

The decree, on November 8, called for all the hostile countries to begin peace negotiations as soon as possible. The Western Powers, angry at the loss of their Russian ally, made no response. The

German troops file onto a steamship to make their way home. Most would face further fighting on the Western Front.

Germans, meanwhile, eager to transfer their forces to the Western Front, announced their readiness to negotiate. Throughout November Leon Trotsky, people's commissar for foreign affairs, repeatedly asked the warring states to agree to a truce. The Western Powers remained silent.

An unusual delegation

Filled with revolutionary passion, the Bolshevik leaders insisted that the initial peace discussions include representatives of all social groups. Thus the Bolshevik delegation included peasants, sailors, soldiers, women, and workers along with party members. This group went to meet with a team of high-ranking German generals.

Negotiations began on December 3 at the German army headquarters in Brest-Litovsk, a city on the present-day border of Poland and Belarus. At first the Germans did not know what to make of their counterparts. At official dinners one of the Russian workers was not sure whether to use his knife or his fork. And the peasant representative amused his hosts: When asked which alcohol he preferred to drink with his meal, he requested the strongest.

The real negotiations, however, proved to be no laughing matter for the Bolsheviks. Their call for certain withdrawals of German troops met with a flat refusal, as did the proposal for a truce on all fronts. After all, said the Germans, the Bolsheviks represented no authority but themselves.

Despite their disappointment at not securing a general armistice, Russia ended the war against Germany on December 5, 1917, by signing a 12-day armistice. It was also agreed that a peace conference would open on December 22. It appeared that the war on the Eastern Front was over.

The Treaty of
BREST-LITOVSK

Desperate for peace, the Bolsheviks would accept almost any terms from the Central Powers. But when the Germans announced they would annex Poland, Lenin's men resisted.

The Treaty of Brest-Litovsk, signed reluctantly by Russia's Bolshevik government on March 3, 1918.

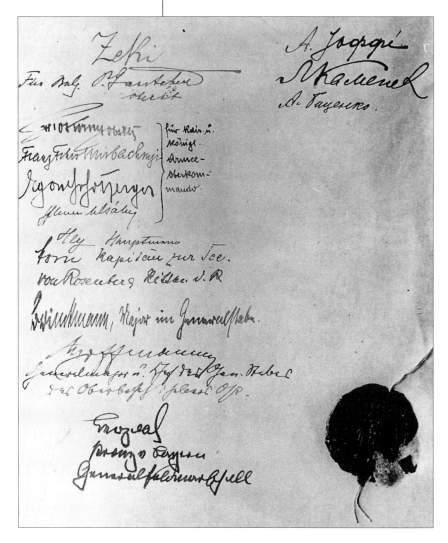

Both sides at the negotiating table at Brest-Litovsk, the town to the west of the front line where the Germans had their headquarters, had a serious desire for peace. In fact Lenin believed that it would be better to sign a bad peace than have none at all. He knew that the masses supported his Bolshevik government only because it was antiwar.

At the same time, the Germans knew that revolution had left Russia's economy, army, and transportation network in a state of collapse. There would be no stopping a German offensive eastward. Yet they could not push Russia too far. Germany needed to transfer troops from the east to the west for an offensive in France before American reinforcements arrived. The longer peace was delayed in the east, the slimmer Germany's chances of victory in the west.

As the talks began in December 1917, things seemed to go well for the Russians. Their opponents agreed to the Bolshevik peace without annexations or compensation for losses. But a few days later the Germans announced, much to the Bolsheviks' horror, that "annexation" did not apply to Poland or the Baltic lands. The first phase of the negotiations ended.

When talks began again on January 8, 1918, Leon Trotsky headed the Bolshevik delegation. He tried to delay the conference in the hope that the revolution would spread to Germany and Austria. But in mid-January the Germans simply told the

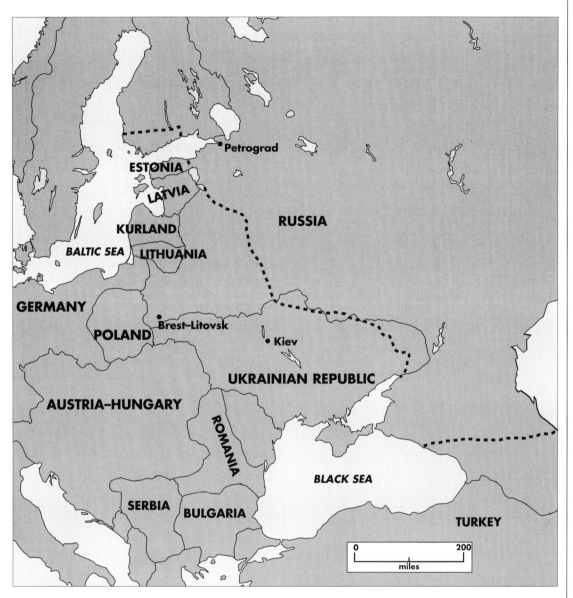

ESTONIA

Petrograd

LATVIA

KURLAND

RUSSIA

BALTIC SEA   LITHUANIA

GERMANY

Brest-Litovsk

POLAND

Kiev

UKRAINIAN REPUBLIC

AUSTRIA-HUNGARY

ROMANIA

BLACK SEA

SERBIA   BULGARIA

TURKEY

0   200
miles

A map shows the division of Russia after the Treaty of Brest-Litovsk. The dotted line shows the furthest extent of Russian territory occupied by the Central Powers before the end of the war in the west in November 1918.

Below: Herr von Kühlmann, German foreign minister, signing the peace treaty at Brest-Litovsk.

Bolsheviks that the territory occupied by the German army would not be given up.

In February Trotsky announced that the Bolsheviks refused the Central Powers' terms. Germany then informed Russia that the two countries were again at war. Lenin threatened to resign if the treaty was not signed. The Bolsheviks finally signed the peace on March 3, 1918. With it Russia lost 26 percent of its population, 60 percent of its European territory, 73 percent of its iron industry, and 75 percent of its coalfields. But at least it was finally out of the war.

The Collapse of AUSTRIA-HUNGARY

Unconvinced by Austro-Hungarian Emperor Karl I's peace initiatives, the Allies would instead support the Slavic peoples of the empire, and watch the Hapsburg monarchy collapse.

An Austrian deserter faces a court martial. Desertion became increasingly common as the empire's armies faced defeat on other fronts.

Far right: Refugees from the empire's farflung corners retreated on Austria. These refugees are in a camp guarded by Austrian soldier.

Emperor Karl I of Austria-Hungary was in a difficult position. The Allies had rejected his peace proposals. And his empire was still dependent on Germany. Karl found his options to salvage the monarchy's prestige diminishing each day. Events would continue to work against him into 1918.

Austria-Hungary launched its final attempt to crush the Italians in June 1918. The offensive might have succeeded had it not been for heavy rains that hampered the Austrian advance. After ten days of fighting the Austrian armies had lost more than 140,000 troops, with no conquered territory to show for it. The setback prompted Karl to seek peace yet again.

This time, however, his initiative fell on deaf ears: By now the Allies did not trust the Dual Monarchy. After the Hapsburg monarchy's previous failed attempt at peace, Britain, France, and America assumed that Karl was counting on Germany's total victory and would not agree to a separate peace. Their assumption was confirmed in June, when the Austrians sent troops to bolster German commander Ludendorff's offensive in the west.

Supporting the Slavs

The Allies decided that if Austria could not be separated from Germany, it should be destroyed. The opponents of Austria therefore gave their support to the Austro-Hungarian empire's national minorities – Poles, Czechs, Slovaks, and the peoples of the Balkans, and also the empire's weaker partners, the Hungarians. The administration of United States President Woodrow Wilson endorsed this intention on June 28, 1918, when it announced that "all branches of the Slav race should be completely freed from German and Austrian rule."

On October 16, in an attempt to keep the monarchy intact, Karl issued a manifesto proclaiming the conversion of his Austrian holdings into a federated country, where all peoples would have equal rights. But it was too late. Karl's announcement came at the same time as Czechoslovakia was proclaiming its own independence.

The collapse of the Hapsburgs

Karl's manifesto also allowed the Poles to join an independent Polish state. They were already doing so. Defeated, Karl abdicated as emperor on November 11. Five days later Count Mihály Károlyi formed a new government in Hungary. It released itself from its allegiance to the Hapsburg crown and declared Hungary a republic. The collapse of the Hapsburg monarchy, which had ruled the Czech and Hungarian lands for nearly 400 years, was complete.

alternatives

What if the leaders of the Dual Monarchy had granted equal political rights to the country's ethnic minorities? Would that have been enough to save the state from disintegration in 1918? Perhaps the Slavic peoples would have agreed to remain as part of Austria-Hungary if the emperor had created a federal state before 1914. But the Hungarians had stopped this scheme and their leaders did all that they could to maintain Hungary's dominance. As a result, when the Slavs of the empire had their chance to leave in 1918 in the wake of the empire's defeat, they had no reason to stay.

HOME FRONT

Austria-Hungary

WAR PROFILES

Mihály Károlyi 1875–1955
Hungarian premier
One of the few true liberals among the Hungarian ruling elites, Count Károlyi favored universal suffrage and the redistribution of large landed estates. He also admired Western democracies, and traveled to France and Britain just before the war to seek cooperation against the growth of German power. Upon his return home, however, he pledged full support to the Hungarian war effort.

In 1916 Károlyi formed a small political party that called for political and social reforms. He became the first premier of the Hungarian republic in October 1918, and president from January to March 1919. But then a Communist government took over, forcing Károlyi into exile. He spent most of the rest of his life outside Hungary.

The ASSASSINATION of the CZAR

The Bolsheviks' brutal killing of Nicholas II and his family shocked the world and helped to foster anti-Bolshevik feeling.

In the summer of 1918 Bolshevik troops were still holding Czar Nicholas II and his family under arrest. After surviving the October Revolution of 1917 in Tobolsk, the royal family had been transferred to Ekaterinburg, a city in Siberia, in April. Here the former czar and his wife Alexandra were confined to a building known as the Ipatiev House, together with their four daughters – Olga, Tatiana, Marie, and Anastasia – and their son, Aleksei, as well as the family doctor and three servants. Here they would spend their final weeks.

At first the new Bolshevik government did not know what to do with the former czar. Some members thought that Nicholas might somehow be forced to endorse the Treaty of Brest-Litovsk, which would deflect blame for the agreement's harsh terms away from the Bolsheviks.

Yet an advance of the Whites – anti-Bolshevik forces – and the Czechoslovak

Czar Nicholas II and his family: Czarina Alexandra sits to the Tsar's right. His children, from left to right are Marie, 19; Tatiana, 21; Olga, 22; and Anastasia, 17. The young heir to the throne, Aleksei, 13, sits at the front of the picture. A widespread revolt forced the weak yet autocratic Nicholas to abdicate in March 1917.

Legion toward Ekaterinburg in early July apparently prompted the Bolshevik leadership to change its mind. The last thing Lenin's government needed was the reappearance of the imperial family, around which opponents to Bolshevism could rally. On the other hand it could be that the the government used the approach of the Whites as a convenient excuse to be rid of the Romanovs for good.

A brutal end

Around midnight on July 16, 1918, a Bolshevik officer, Yakov Yurovsky, ordered the Romanov's doctor to prepare the royal family to move to the basement of Ipatiev House. Yurovsky claimed that the approach of the White forces had caused unrest in the city, and that the family would be safer downstairs.

The czar had to carry Aleksei down the stairs: His son was weak, since he suffered from hemophilia, a blood defect. The basement was a dank, bare room, lit only by guttering lamps and a single lantern. When the family and servants assembled in the basement, the officer directed them to line up against the back wall. He stated that a photograph was to be taken in order to show that they had not escaped.

Then, instead of a photographer, 11 men filed in, armed with revolvers. Yurovsky read the execution order. Just as Nicholas began to try and protect his family, the soldiers and the officer opened fire. The former czar, his wife, his oldest daughter, the family doctor, and two of the three servants were killed instantly.

The younger children took longer to die: Bullets fired at the younger girls seemed to bounce off them, terrifying the soldiers. They were wearing corsets with diamonds sewn into the material, which acted like a shield. The executioners continued to fire,

The house in which the Czar and his family were murdered by Bolsheviks in Ekaterinburg, Russia.

Below: Anastasia (second from right) with her sisters (left to right) Maria, Tatiana, and Olga, in St. Petersburg in 1914.

Below: The room in which the Romanovs were shot. The wall is scarred with bullet holes and bayonet-thrusts.

Mystery survivor?

Confusion over the fate of the Romanovs led to rumors that they were still alive. Nicholas himself had allegedly been seen in London, and again in Rome, where he was supposedly being hidden by the pope. All sorts of pretenders surfaced, ranging from the bizarre – a woman who worked as a prostitute in Istanbul claiming to be the Grand Duchess Tatiana – to the ridiculous: a Polish spy who maintained that he was the Czarevich, or prince, Aleksei.

The best known case was that of Anna Anderson, who claimed to be the Grand Duchess Anastasia. Turning up in Berlin in 1920, she insisted that she had survived the shooting at Ekaterinburg. She was apparently transported across Russia by a Polish soldier, and had come to Berlin to seek the help of her mother's sister, Princess Irene of Prussia.

The alleged grand duchess became the source of violent disagreement in Russian emigré circles, some supporting her, others denouncing her. She ultimately became a naturalized American citizen, and died on February 12, 1984. Ten years later, using a piece of intestine taken from the alleged Anastasia, and blood donated by the British royal family – who are distant relations to the Romanovs – a British forensic team determined once and for all that Anna Anderson was a fraud.

however, finishing the job without having to reload. The only survivor, a servant, was bayonetted to death, and even a pet dog was brutally killed.

Dumping the bodies

The officer in charge, Yurovsky, noted that the whole bloody scene lasted 20 minutes. The bodies were taken secretly to a nearby forest around 12 miles north of Ekaterinburg. There they were seared with sulfuric acid, burned, and dumped in an abandoned mine shaft.

It was a long time before the Bolsheviks admitted what they had done. The Bolshevik government did not admit to the murders of Alexandra and the children until 1926. They did not hide their pride in ridding the country of the hated czar, however, and even rewarded the perpetrators. Yurovsky was awarded the Inspectorship of Life Insurance for Ekaterinburg Province, a pension, and a large house.

Establishing the truth

The location of the remains of the Romanovs remained a secret until 1979, when a local geologist and a Moscow film maker discovered the graves. Yet the find was kept secret, and only after the fall of the Soviet Union in 1991 was permission given to exhume the bodies.

An examination of the bodies by a team of Russian specialists, and DNA tests undertaken by British scientists, seem to establish beyond doubt that these were indeed the remains of the Romanov royal family. While the Russian Orthodox Church establishes the details – church officials want yet another DNA test done by Russian scientists – the bodies remain in a morgue in Siberia, awaiting a burial more befitting royalty.

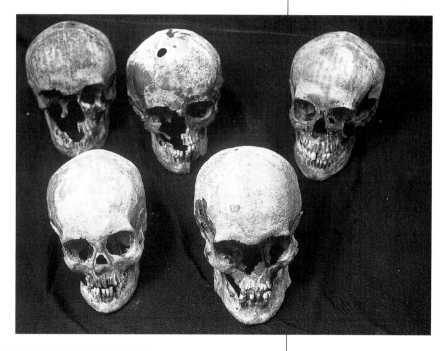

Skulls of the czar and his family.

Russian emigrés

The final defeat of the White movement toward the end of 1920 prompted hundreds of thousands of refugees to flee their homeland. The exact number of emigrés who left because of the revolutionary upheavals in Russia is unknown: estimates range from several hundred thousand people up to one million.

The Soviet government was hurt by the emigration of professionals and intellectuals. A large number of scholars and scientists took up positions abroad. The West benefitted from their expertise and knowledge while the Soviet economy suffered from a lack of qualified managers and supervisors. And the cultural world in Soviet Russia suffered the loss of musicians like Rachmaninov and Stravinsky, and artists like Chagall.

SET INDEX

Volume numbers appear in **bold**. Page references in *italics* refer to pictures on pages which do not have text on the subject. Map references also are in *italics*. Individual weapons are all listed under the heading *weapons*.

Africa **1** 69; **2** 42-5, 70-1
  campaigns against German colonies **2** 102-5; **7** 118-19
  colonialism **1** 71-2, 75-7, 79
air aces **7** 40
air battles **5** 42; **7** 36-41
air raids **3** 38-40, 42; **4** 105, 106-7
  Gotha raids **5** 74
  Oberndorf **4** 101
Aisne, battles of the
  1914 **2** 72-4, *73*, 76-7
  1917 **5** 40-1, *41*, 43, 44-5
  1918 **7** 44-6, 48-9
Albert I, King of the Belgians **1** 35; **2** 12-13
Alexander II, Czar of Russia **1** 44-5, *46*, 47
Alexander III, Czar of Russia **1** 45
Alexeiev, Mikhail Vasilevich **6** 57, 62
Algeciras Conference 1906 **1** *79*
Allenby, Edmund **5** 25, 33-5, 110
  Beersheba **5** 104-5
  Jerusalem, capture of **5** 108-11
  Megiddo offensive **7** 86-7
Alsace-Lorraine **1** 11, 22; **2** 26-9, *29*; **8** 38
American Expeditionary Force *see* U.S. Army (AEF).
Amiens, battles of **7** 26-7, 66-8
Anthony, Susan B. **5** 12
anti-Semitism **4** 99; **8** 95, 97
Anzac Cove, Gallipoli **3** 71-2, 73
Anzacs **3** 70-3
  in France **7** 67, 74, 96
Arabs **3** *31*; **4** 62
  revolt against Turkey 1916 **4** 58-61, 63-4
Ardennes, battle of **2** 30-1
Armenia, massacres in **4** 18-19
armies **1** 104
  see also individual countries' armies.
armistices **7** 112-14, 116-17, *117*
  Austria-Hungary **7** 101

Russia & Germany **6** 111
arms **1** 80-5; **3** 48-9
  development **8** 69
  production **3** 42, 88-91; **4** 92-5
  stockpiles **2** 76; **8** 75-6
Arras, battle of **2** 77-8; **5** 32-5
artillery **1** 80-1; **3** 14-15; **7** 30-1
  creeping barrages **4** 27; **5** 41
  hurricane of fire **6** 51
  Hutier tactics **5** 102, 115; **6** 99
  see also weapons.
Artois, battles of **3** 84-7, 96-8
arts **8** 100-7, 114
Atlantic, battle *see* U-boats.
August 1914 (A. Solzhenitsyn) **6** 21
Australian troops **3** 70, *72, 73*
  in France **7** 67, 74, 96
Austria-Hungary **1** 10, 36-7, 37, 39; **6** 28-9; **8** 44, *45*
  declarations of war **1** 108; **2** 38; **6** 10
  defeat **6** 114-15
  Germany, tensions with **6** 57, 68-9
  home front **6** 10-11, 28-9, 78
  nationalism **1** 89, 98; **6** 33, 52-3
  peace initiatives **6** 88-9
  peace treaties **8** 41, 44, *45*
  Poland, manifesto for **6** 76-7
  St. Germain, Treaty of **8** 41
  Serbia, invasion of **2** 38-41, *39*
  Serbia, ultimatum to **1** 98-103
  Yugoslavia, creation of **5** 88-9; **8** 41
Austro-German armies **6** 57, 73
  Caporetto **5** 100-3, *101*
  Romania **4** 89-91
  Serbia **3** 102-5, *103*
Austro-Hungarian armies **1** *104*, 105-6, 108, 117
  demobilization **8** 20-1, 22
  desertion **3** 17
Austro-Hungarian armies battles
  Belgrade **1** 108; **2** 40, 114-15
  Drina River **2** 38-9, 68-9
  Isonzo **3** 92-5, *93*; **4** 84-5; **5** 52-3
  Montenegro **4** 10-11
  Piave **7** 58-61
  Przemysl **6** 30-2, *31*, 49
  Trentino **4** 48-51
  Vittorio Veneto **7** 98-9, 101
  Zamosc-Komarów **6** 24-7
Averescu, Alexandru **4** 90

B

Baghdad, fall of **5** 20-1

Baker, Josephine **8** 87, 89
balance of power, 1914 **1** 74-9, 91
  arms race **1** 80-5
Baldwin, Stanley **8** 81-2
Balfour Declaration **4** 62, 63-4
Balkans **1** 39, 86-8, 89
  Yugoslavia, creation of **5** 88-9
Balkans, battles
  Belgrade **1** 108; **2** 40, 114-15
  Drina River **2** 38-9, 68-9
  Montenegro **4** 10-11
  Romania **4** 86-7, 89-91; **5** 82-3
  Salonika 1915 **3** 106-9, *107*
  Salonika 1916 **4** 86-7
  Salonika 1917 **5** 48-9, *48*
  Serbia, fall of **3** 102-5, *103*, 107-8
  Serbia, invasion of **2** 38-41, *39*
  Vardar **7** 84-5
Ball, Albert **7** 38
Baltic republics **8** 44, *45*, 73
Baruch, Bernard **5** 30, 31
"Battalion of Death" **3** 35; **6** 74, *75*, 96
Battle of the Somme (movie) **4** 76-7
battles *see* individual battles.
Beatty, Sir David **2** 48, 51; **3** 18-19, 21
Beersheba, battle of **5** 104-5
Belgium **1** 32-5, *33*; **3** 116-17
  food aid **3** 51; **4** 37
  invasion of **2** 12-13, 15-17
  neutrality **1** 34, 100, 112-13
Belgrade **1** 108; **2** 40, 114-15
Belleau Wood, battle of **7** 54-6
Beneš, Edvard **6** 53, 86, 87; **8** 46
Bethmann Hollweg, Theobald von **4** 41, 112-13
  July Crisis 1914 **1** 101-3, 108-9
Bismarck, Otto von **1** 10-12, 76, 79
black Americans **2** 52; **5** 84-5, 86-7; **8** 62
  in the army **7** 82-3
Black Hand gang **1** 93, 94
blockades, naval **2** 52
  North Sea **3** 44-7, 45; **4** 52-5, *53*
  Northern barrage **7** 22-3
  prize rules **3** 46-7; **4** 40
  U-boat blockade **3** 47, 82-3; **4** 38-41, 55; **5** 18-19, 50-1
"Bloody April" **5** 42
Boer revolt **2** 70-1
Boer wars **1** 76, 77
Bolsheviks **6** 82
Bosnia-Herzegovina **1** 39, 79
Botha, Louis **2** 70, 71; **7** 119
Boxer rising **1** 63, 64, 65

breakthrough tactics **6** 73
Breslau **2** 98, 101
Brest-Litovsk, Treaty of **6** 112-13, *113*; **8** 73
Britain **1** 16-19, *17*, 21, 78
  air raids **3** 38-40, 42; **4** 105-7
  arms supplies **3** 88-91
  Atlantic convoys **5** 50-1
  colonialism **1** 18, 19, *68*, 69-71, 73
  declaration of war **2** 22
  depression **8** 82-3
  East Coast raids **3** 19
  fading empire **1** 18
  General Strike **8** 82, 84-5
  home front **2** 22-5; **4** 81-3
  invasion threat **3** 41
  Irish home rule **4** 42-5; **8** 52, 79
  Jarrow Crusade **8** 82-3
  leisure activities **5** 76-7
  Military Service acts **4** 81-2
  opium trade **1** 69-70
  postwar **8** 78-83
  rationing **7** 16-19
  response to Wilson note **4** 117-18
  trade with U.S. **3** 48, 49
  Triple Entente **1** 21, 24
  U-boat blockade **4** 38-41; **5** 18-19, 50-1
  women's suffrage **1** 20; **8** 80
British armies **1** 107, 116, *118*, 119; **4** 74-5
  BEF **2** 31, 33-4, 54, 64, 66-7, 69, 78, 84-9; **3** 24-7
  colonial troops **2** 63; **3** 85; **4** 12-16, *17*; **8** 23
  demobilization **8** 23-5, 26-7
  discipline **5** 46-7
  friendships **4** 75, 79; **5** 72-3
  leave **5** 80-1
  mobilization **1** *114*, 115; **2** 23
  officers and men **4** 74-5, 78-9
  recruitment **2** 22, 64-7; **4** 43, 80-2
British armies battles
  Aisne 1914 **2** 72-4, *73*, 76-7
  Aisne 1918 **7** 44-6, 48-9
  Amiens **7** 26-7, 66-8
  Arras **2** 77-8; **5** 32-5
  Artois **3** 84-7, 96-8
  Baghdad, fall of **5** 20-1
  Beersheba **5** 104-5
  Cambrai **5** 112-15
  Dublin rising **4** 42, 43-4, 46
  Gallipoli **3** 68-73, *69*
  Gaza **5** 24-5, 104-5
  German West Africa **2** 42-3, 45; **7** 118-19

Index of BIOGRAPHIES

Picture credits

GLOSSARY

artillery barrage – a heavy bombardment of explosive shells onto enemy positions, often used to prepare for an infantry attack.

bayonet – a sharp blade attached to the muzzle of a rifle and used for hand-to-hand fighting.

blockade – the use of warships and mines to cut off an enemy's sea trade.

chief of staff – the military head of an army.

depth charge – a waterproof explosive that detonates underwater to destroy enemy submarines.

division – a military unit of between 10,000 and 17,000 soldiers and support troops.

draft – large-scale selection of civilians for compulsory military scrvicc.

fortress – a large, heavily defended permanent fortification, often surrounding a town or city.

grenade – a small missile containing explosives or chemicals, such as poison gas or a smoke producer.

home front – the wartime activity of civilians away from the battle fronts.

infantry – a branch of an army trained and equipped to fight and move on foot.

intelligence – information about enemy positions and plans.

land mine – an explosive charge that is buried just beneath the surface of the ground. The land mine explodes if a person stands on it or if a tank drives over the top.

mobilization – the assembly and preparation of a country's armed forces for war.

mortar – a short, portable artillery weapon that fires heavy shells in an arc over short distances.

No Man's Land – the ground between the trenches of opposing forces.

"over the top" – the name given to climbing out of one's own trenches to advance.

propaganda – information designed to influcncc public opinion or damage enemy morale.

reconnaissance – a survey of enemy territory to gather intelligence.

reparations – payments made by a defeated nation in compensation for costs and damages sustained during war.

reserves – a body of troops which is held back from action for later use.

salient – an outward bulge in an army's front line which has to be defended on three exposed sides.

sea mine – a waterproof explosive charge that is placed on or beneath the surface of the water. The mine explodes if a vessel touches it or passes near by.

shell shock – a psychological trauma suffered by soldiers under prolonged enemy fire.

shrapnel – flying fragments of a bomb, mine, or shell that can cause serious or fatal injuries.

stormtroops – soldiers trained and armed to break through enemy lines after an artillery barrage.

strategic bombing – air raids designed to damage an enemy's military, economic, or industrial capacity.

theater of war – an area of land, sea, or air that is directly involved in military actions.

trenches – long, deep ditches dug in the ground for use as defensive fortifications.

trench foot – an infection of the feet caused by cold and wet trench conditions.

U-boat – a term for German and Austrian submarines. The word comes from the German *Unterseeboot*, meaning "submarine."

Zeppelin – a rigid airship constructed of a frame covered by material and filled with gas.

BIBLIOGRAPHY

History

Brogan, Hugh, *The Pelican History of the United States of America.* New York: Penguin USA, 1987.

Bruce, Anthony, *An Illustrated Companion to the First World War.* New York: Penguin USA, 1990.

Gilbert, Martin, *First World War.* New York: Henry Holt & Co., 1996.

Gilbert, Martin, *Atlas of the First World War.* New York: Oxford University Press, 1994.

Gray, Randal, and Christopher Argyle, eds., *Chronicle of the First World War,* 2 vols. Mechanicsburg, PA: Stackpole, 1991.

Joll, James, *The Origins of the First World War.* New York: Longman, 1984.

Joll, James, *Europe Since 1870: An International History.* New York: HarperCollins College Publishers.

MacDonald, Lyn, *1914–1918: Voices and Images of the Great War.* New York: Penguin USA, 1991.

Macksey, Kenneth, *The Penguin Encyclopedia of Weapons & Military Technology from Pre-History to the Present Day.* New York: Penguin USA, 1994.

Pope, Stephen, and Wheal, Elizabeth-Anne, *Dictionary of the First World War.* New York: St. Martin's Press, 1995.

Reed, John Silas, *Ten Days that Shook the World.* New York: Bantam, 1992.

Thomas, Gill, *Life on All Fronts: Women in the First World War.* New York: Cambridge University Press, 1989.

Tuchmann, Barbara W., *The Guns of August.* New York: Ballantine, 1994.

Weintraub, Stanley, *A Stillness Heard Round the World. The End of the Great War: November 1918.* New York: Oxford University Press, 1987.

Winter, Denis, *Death's Men: Soldiers of the Great War.* New York: Penguin USA, 1985.

Winter, Jay, *The Great War.* New York: Penguin USA, 1996.

Fiction, Memoirs, and Poetry

Brittain, Vera, *A Testament of Youth.* New York: Viking, 1994.

Brown, Malcolm, *The Imperial War Museum Book of the First World War: A Great Conflict Recalled in Previously Unpublished Letters, Diaries & Memoirs.* Philadelphia: Trans-Atlantic Publications Inc., 1993.

Dos Passos, John, *1919.* New York: Amereon Ltd.

Faulkner, William, *A Soldier's Pay.* New York: Liveright, 1990.

Graves, Robert, *Goodbye to All That.* Providence, RI: Berghahn Books, 1995.

Hašek, Jaroslav, *The Good Soldier Švejk.* New York: Robert Bentley Publishing, 1980.

Hemingway, Ernest, *A Farewell to Arms.* New York: Simon & Schuster, 1995.

MacArthur, Douglas, *Reminiscences.* New York: Da Capo, 1985.

Remarque, Erich Maria, *All Quiet on the Western Front.* New York: Barron, 1984.

Sassoon, Siegfried, *Collected Poems, 1908–1953.* Winchester, MA: Faber & Faber.

Sassoon, Siegfried, *Memoirs of an Infantry Officer.* Winchester, MA: Faber & Faber, 1965.

Solzhenitsyn, Aleksandr, *August 1914.* New York: Farrar, Strauss & Giroux Inc, 1989.

Owen, Wilfred, *Collected Poems.* New York: New Directions, 1964.

Vaughan, Edwin, *Some Desperate Glory.* New York: Henry Holt & Co., 1988

Wilder, Amos N., *Armageddon Revisited. A World War I Journal.* New Haven, CT: Yale University Press, 1994.

Yeats, W.B., *The Collected Poems.* New York: Simon and Schuster, 1996.